The Will
to Empower

The Will to Empower

Democratic Citizens and Other Subjects

Barbara Cruikshank

CORNELL UNIVERSITY PRESS

ITHACA AND LONDON

First published 1999 by Cornell University Press
First printing, Cornell Paperbacks, 1999

Cornell University Press strives to use environmentally responsible suppliers and materials to the fullest extent possible in the publishing of its books. Such materials include vegetable-based, low-VOC inks and acid-free papers that are recycled, totally chlorine-free, or partly composed of nonwood fibers. For further information, visit our website at www.cornell press.cornell.edu.

Printed in the United States of America

Library of Congress Cataloging-in-Publication Data
Cruikshank, Barbara.
     The will to empower : democratic citizens and other subjects / Barbara Cruikshank.
          p.   cm.
     Includes bibliographical references and index.
     ISBN 0-8014-3480-7 (cloth : alk. paper).   ISBN 0-8014-8599-1 (pbk. : alk. paper)
     1. Political participation — United States.   2. Democracy — United States.
     3. Power (Social sciences) — United States.   I. Title.
     JK1764.C78   1999   98-46489
     324.6′3′0973 — dc21

CLOTH PRINTING

10   9   8   7   6   5   4   3   2   1

PAPERBACK PRINTING

10   9   8   7   6   5   4   3   2

Contents

Acknowledgments

This book is dedicated to Peter Schwartz, who told me I could be a political theorist. I believed him.

During its production I incurred a great many personal debts which are a pleasure to bear. The first is to Judith Halberstam, whose faith and financial support sustained my earliest efforts, even when she wasn't sure what I had to say. I am most grateful to Judith for teaching me how to live well. For friendship, camaraderie, and her intelligence, I owe Carla Bates more respect and gratitude than my prose could ever muster. I rely upon Janet Lukehart and Marta Schultz for all good things; without them I could not have written this book. I am grateful to Beth Jones for her bravura, research assistance, and last-minute rescues. Jenny Robertson put her muscle into the later stages of the production. Lisa Henderson and Janice Irvine helped to keep it all in perspective week by week. Linda Rahm gave me something to look forward to after the book was finished.

Thomas Dumm read the entire manuscript and gave critical advice at many turns; my intellectual debt to his own work is enormous. Diane Brooks, Neta Crawford, Louis Howe, Sue Hyatt, Shane Phelan, Jenny Robertson, Nikolas Rose, Sanford Schram, Jackie Urla, and Mariana Valverde read chapters, offered criticism, and encouraged my labors. Also, many thanks to Nikolas Rose and the others who sustain the History of the Present Research Network.

Under the tutelage of Mary G. Dietz I learned what it meant to be taken seriously and that intellectual rigor does not mean sacrificing what one has to say. Thanks also to Sara Evans, Edwin Fogelman, Lawrence Jacobs, and Paula Rabinowitz for criticism and encouragement. The University of Minnesota Graduate School Wallace Fellowship provided early research support.

Women, Work and Welfare, a welfare rights organization in Minneapolis, offered me and many other women the opportunity to cut our political teeth. For their political savvy, for all our infighting, and especially for teaching me to suspect my own will to empower, I am grateful to Betty Christenson, Kelly Pitts, Barbara Jones, Cheri Honkala, and Carla Bates.

Finally, to Alison Shonkwiler, a generous editor and a patient reader, many thanks.

Permission has been granted to use in revised versions the following three previously published articles: "Revolutions Within: Self-Government and Self-Esteem," *Economy and Society* 22, no. 3 (1993): 327–344; "The Will to Empower: Technologies of Citizenship and the War on Poverty," *Socialist Review* 23, no. 4 (1994): 29–55; "Welfare Queens: Policing by the Numbers," in *Tales of the State: Readings on the Legendary Character of Public Policy*, ed. Sanford Schram and Phillip Neisser, (Lanham, MD : Rowman & Littlefield, 1997), 113–124.

The Will
to Empower

Introduction
Small Things

A meticulous observation of detail, and at the same time a political awareness of these small things, for the control and use of man, emerge through
the classical age bearing with them a whole set of techniques, a whole cor-
pus of methods and knowledge, descriptions, plans, and data. And from
such trifles, no doubt, the man of modern humanism was born.

MICHEL FOUCAULT

The popular mind in fact doubles the deed: it posits the same event as
cause and then a second time as its effect.

FRIEDRICH NIETZSCHE

For my part, I should be inclined to think that liberty is less necessary in
great matters than in tiny ones if I imagined that one could ever be safe
in the enjoyment of one sort of freedom without the other.

ALEXIS DE TOCQUEVILLE

In reformist and democratic discourses, citizenship and self-government are tirelessly put forward as solutions to poverty, political apathy,
powerlessness, crime, and innumerable other problems. But that stance
obscures any political awareness of how citizens are brought into being; it
obscures the will to empower embedded in posing democracy as a solution.
I argue that democratic citizenship is less a solution to political problems
than a strategy of government.

Individual subjects are transformed into citizens by what I call technologies of citizenship: discourses, programs, and other tactics aimed at
making individuals politically active and capable of self-government. Examples might include a neighborhood organizing campaign, an empower-

ment program, safe-sex education, a shelter for battered women, social service programs promoting self-help, self-sufficiency, or self-esteem, or a radically democratic social movement.

I see these technologies of citizenship, however well intentioned, as modes of constituting and regulating citizens: that is, strategies for governing the very subjects whose problems they seek to redress — the powerless, the apathetic, or those at risk. Although I am deeply sympathetic to the project of radical or participatory democracy, I am skeptical that such a project presents an answer to questions of power, inequality, and political participation. Like any mode of government, democracy both enables and constrains the possibilities for political action. Democratic modes of governance are not *necessarily* more or less dangerous, free, or idealistic than any other. Even democratic self-government is still a mode of exercising power — in this case, over oneself. Like government more generally, self-government can swing between the poles of tyranny and absolute liberty. One can govern one's own *or* others' lives well or badly.

The only sure thing, in my somewhat Machiavellian view, is that solutions to the problems of politics will not be found in a particular form of government, in a theory, in human reason, or in some truth; they will be found, for better or worse, in more politics. If poststructural political theory has a hidden foundation, it is that power and political conflict are as ubiquitous, as commonplace, as dangerous *and* as productive behind the bedroom door as they are in the legislature. Conflict and struggle are a permanent historical condition. Or, as Michel Foucault so famously put it, "everything is dangerous," even democracy.[1]

I investigate the familiar problematics of democratic theory — inequalities of power, participation, resistance, knowledge, and citizenship — through the insights of feminist and poststructural political theory. Two notions, that power relations are ubiquitous and that subjectivity is both enabled and constrained by relations of power, help to make these problematics thinkable in new ways attuned to the contingencies of politics. Democratic theories, I argue, are best understood as constitutive discourses that contribute to solidifying what it is possible to think, say, do, and be democratically.

I want neither to overstate nor to neglect the dangers of democracy. I do not seek to disclose some evil hidden away in democratic discourses; they are both enabling and constraining. The will to empower others and oneself is neither a bad nor a good thing. It is political; the will to empower contains the twin possibilities of domination and freedom. In Chapter 2 I trace the origins of the will to empower to the shift from Christian charity to social work as a guiding principle of philanthropy in the nineteenth century; in Chapters 2 and 3 I explain that the will to empower is expressed in peculiar kinds of governing relationships which by definition erase the traces of the philanthropist's will, especially the will to self-help and self-empowerment. My goal, however, is not to indict the will to empower but to show that even the most democratic modes of government entail power relationships that are both voluntary and coercive.

Two questions drive the discussion that follows. The first is, what are the problems to which democratic participation is posed as the solution? Most consistently, what I have found is that democratic participation and self-government are regarded as solutions to the lack of something: for example, a lack of power, of self-esteem, of coherent self-interest, or of political consciousness. Along with social service programs, philanthropy, and some kinds of political associations, participatory democratic discourse is preoccupied with the subjects who do not rebel against their own exploitation and inequality, who fail to act in their own interests, and who do not participate politically even though free to do so. Indeed, the analytical and normative vocabularies of democratic theory are replete with formulations expressing what is not there: "powerlessness," "non-participation," "non-decision," and "counterfactuals."

The second question is, by what means is the capacity, power, consciousness, or subjectivity proper to democratic participation and self-government infused into citizens? How does the will to empower work; how are individuals empowered, transformed from apathetic and powerless subjects into active, participatory citizens? How is subjugation transformed into subjectivity? Are the means by which citizens are constituted themselves democratic?

The first of my two main arguments is that democratic modes of governance and social scientific ways of knowing (re)produce citizens who are capable of governing themselves, of acting in their own interests and in solidarity with others. Citizens are not born; they are made. I explain the political significance of the ways social scientific knowledge is operationalized in techniques, programs, and strategies for governing, shaping, and guiding those who are held to exhibit some specified lack. Throughout the book I use examples of the practical role played by social science in applying the liberal arts of government.

To be clear, I do not mean that citizens are socially constructed by *the* government. My argument turns on distinguishing between the state and governance. By "the state" I mean the liberal, representative, electoral, administrative, legislative, and judicial institutions and practices articulated within the confines of a liberal constitutional framework. By "governance," I mean what Michel Foucault called "the conduct of conduct" or "governmentality," forms of action and relations of power that aim to guide and shape (rather than force, control, or dominate) the actions of others. In this broad sense, governance includes any program, discourse, or strategy that attempts to alter or shape the actions of others or oneself. It includes but is not limited to programs conducted by the liberal state, for governance can also involve internal and voluntary relations of rule, the ways we act upon ourselves.

Liberal democratic governance is premised not so much upon the autonomy or the rights of individuals as upon their social fabrication as citizens, a fact that is obscured when citizenship is regarded as a solution. The two normative trajectories of liberal democratic thought diverge on the question of whether or not the citizen is inherently rational and self-interested or self-realizing. In either case, however, the liberty of the citizens is understood to be the limit of liberal governance. It is in those cases where individuals do not act in their own self-interest or appear indifferent to their own development as full-fledged citizens that the limit of the liberal state at the threshold of individual rights, liberty, and pursuits must be crossed.

I find that participatory and democratic schemes—what I am calling technologies of citizenship—for correcting the deficiencies of citizens are endemic within liberal democratic societies. Technologies of citizenship operate according to a political rationality for governing people in ways that promote their autonomy, self-sufficiency, and political engagement; in the classic phrase of early philanthropists, they are intended to "help people to help themselves." This is a manner of governing that relies not on institutions, organized violence or state power but on securing the voluntary compliance of citizens. I argue, however, that the autonomy, interests, and wills of citizens are shaped as well as enlisted. Technologies of citizenship do not cancel out the autonomy and independence of citizens but are modes of governance that work upon and through the capacities of citizens to act on their own. Technologies of citizenship are voluntary and coercive at the same time; the actions of citizens are regulated, but only after the capacity to act as a certain kind of citizen with certain aims is instilled. Democratic citizens, in short, are both the effects and the instruments of liberal governance.

Three relatively recent technologies of citizenship are fully treated here in Chapters 3, 4, and 5: Community Action Programs under the Johnson administration; the self-esteem movement; and the reorganization of welfare accounting practices under President Carter which resulted in the emergence of a new kind of citizen — the welfare queen. Below and in Chapter 2, garbage reform and nineteenth-century self-help schemes illustrate the extent to which social reform movements aim at accomplishing through volunteerism and gentle coercion what the liberal state cannot do without using force or violating its limits. Although the scope and impact of a given social reform movement may be short-lived, its techniques for making citizens do not disappear but are reformed or carried over into new programs.

My second overarching argument is that the political itself is continually transformed and reconstituted at the micro-levels of everyday life where citizens are constituted. If power is ubiquitous, as I assert throughout, then it makes no sense to speak of "the political," "the social," "the private," and "the public" as separate domains. The political cannot be clearly demarcated from other domains without excluding some relations of power.[2] Instead of reconceptualizing the political per se, I try to understand how the social transformation of the political opens new possibilities for political action.

I resist the temptation to locate the political only where there is contestation or overt relationships of power. First, I want to avoid the presumption that there is an inside and an outside to politics. Second, in Chapters 1 and 5, I argue that to say something is political only once it is contested is a strategical move that masks the will to empower. For example, in Chapter 5 I find it troubling to say with Nancy Fraser that where there is no overt political resistance, relations of power and inequality have been "depoliticized." To say that welfare and bureaucratic modes of government "depoliticize" the political exclusion of welfare recipients is to mistake the absence of resistance for an absence of politics.

It is not enough to say that recipients are excluded from politics, because, as Judith Butler put a related argument, that "misses the point that the subject is an accomplishment regulated and produced in advance. And as such is fully political; indeed, perhaps most political at the point in which it is claimed to be prior to politics itself."[3] The citizen is an effect and an instrument of political power rather than simply a participant in politics. The measure of democracy is not the extent to which citizens participate in politics rather than stand back in fear or apathy. That is to mistake power for what it excludes rather than what it produces. The critical question for democratic theory is how citizens are constituted by politics and power. To answer that question, one must recognize the contingency of the political itself.

For example, in Chapter 4 on the self-esteem movement, I explain how the self is made into a terrain of political action, a terrain that carries new political possibilities for self-government. In that case, acting upon the self is also a manner of acting politically which self-esteem advocates believe can transform society as a whole. One might be tempted to say that the self-esteem movement "politicizes" the self. To "politicize" self-esteem, however, to bring it into the domain of politics, is to leave politics as it was and simply add something new to it.

I understand social reform movements to do something more profound than carry new issues into the political domain. Social movements transform the political itself; that is, they transform the terrain of political action. Ernesto Laclau and Chantal Mouffe make a similar claim about the unprecedented politicization of the social by new social movements since the 1960s: "What has been exploded is the idea and the reality itself of a unique space of the political. What we are witnessing is a politicization far more radical than any we have known in the past, because it tends to dissolve the distinction between the public and the private."[4] I trace their insight to reform movements in the nineteenth century and so call into question the "newness" of new social movements.

There are two points of departure for this book. The first is democratic theory. The second is the idea of the social — "society as a whole" and "social government" — that developed over the course of the nineteenth century. The social emerged as (1) an object of scientific knowledge (statistics, surveys, the census, and political economy), (2) a set of techniques for indirectly intervening in the lives of the dispossessed (social work, social service, social welfare, economy), and (3) the object of reform movements. A brief account of the historical emergence of the social is given in Chapter 2. What is most important for my purposes is not the history of the social itself but the unique modes of reform and government it made possible.

Once more, to be clear, "the social" is not the space traversed between citizens and the state; it is neither the space of uncoerced association (as in "civil society") nor the space of conformity and domination (as in "social control"). Rather, the social confuses and reconstitutes the boundaries between the personal and the political, the economy and the state, the voluntary and the coercive.

For example, "social problems," given their first systematic treatments at the turn of the twentieth century, define an abstract field of intervention. As Gilles Deleuze put it, the social is a "hybrid domain" made consistent not by its institutions but by its techniques.[5] The novelty of social techniques of government was that they made it possible to target individuals and society as a whole in a single aim. Social government had a new object, to govern what J. A. Hobson in *The Social Problem* (1901) described as "man in society."[6]

The key to understanding the political possibilities that emerged with the social in the nineteenth century is that the term was used both to designate "the whole of society" and to distinguish the poor from the body of society. Mary Poovey suggests that this double usage "allowed social analysts to treat one segment of the population as a special problem at the same time that they could gesture toward the mutual interests that (theoretically) united all parts of the social whole."[7] As Hobson put it in, the "social problem may be set in terms of wealth or terms of want."[8] In either case, any impediment to harmony and progress, including class conflict, needed to be calculated, known, and acted upon. The welfare and progress of society as a whole were linked to solving the poverty of some of its members. Any solution had to be "applied alike to the individual and the social organism, so as to yield a scientific harmony of the claims of Socialism and Individualism."[9]

To extend the reach of power to both at the same time, the political itself had to be reconstituted at the social level, where the individual's liberty was brought into harmony with social progress. That is to say, once the social became the object of reform, agitation, and science, the political lost its spatial association with sovereign power and the state. What mattered most was that "the form of the solution," in Hobson's phrase, be resolved so that it might provide the principles needed by social reformers of all kinds. The form of Hobson's solution to the social problem was "the art of social conduct":

> A satisfactory answer cannot consist in the theoretical solution of a problem; it must lie in the region of social conduct. Not merely saying what should be done, but the doing, is the solution. The reins of Science and Practice are drawn together; a theory of social conduct which shall take cognizance of all the factors will be likewise the art of social conduct.[10]

The theory and the art of social conduct provided reformers with a rationality of government that they carefully distinguished from the state.

The art of social conduct, wrote Hobson, required "marking clearly the operation of those industrial and social forces which make for the larger and more various activities of the state in politics and industry, and those which, on the other hand, directly tend to enlarge the bounds of individual liberty and enterprise."[11] Applying the art of social conduct at the level on which the individual was constituted and regulated meant that power had to find a way into the minute and mundane reaches of the habits, desires, interests, and daily lives of individuals. The art of social conduct was applied to secure the "social cooperation" necessary to keep state intervention to a minimum; in the same step, the sphere of individual liberty was enlarged.

With the advent of the social as the principle of governing individual conduct, power was articulated through the constitution and regulation of individual liberty. Even, or most especially, the smallest details of life came under the terrain of social intervention. Although Hobson argued for the unity of the "Social Question," he also recognized its practical components: "The practical reformer has narrowed the phrase to connote Drink, Sex, Relations, Population, or even Money";[12] he added labor, class conflict, education, and consumption to the list. The unity of the social question, however, was provided by the laws of progress. "'The history of progress is the record of a gradual diminution of Waste.' From this standpoint the Social Question will find its essential unity in the problem of how to deal with human waste."[13]

Waste, taken perhaps more literally than Hobson intended, provides the perfect illustration of how citizens are constituted and regulated and how the political is reconstituted by the arts of social conduct.

George Edwin Waring, a Civil War colonel who became the street-cleaning commissioner of New York City, created the Juvenile Street Cleaning League in the 1890s in order to encourage the public to feel responsible for the disposal of waste. The league — a voluntary association of working class-children that was formed despite the initial suspicion that the children were being used as an informal army of garbage police — was a great success and spread from New York to other cities shortly after the turn of the century. The children, Waring claimed, "are being taught that *government* does not mean merely a policeman to be run away from, but *an influence that touches the life of the people at every point.*"[14] Another way to say the same thing is that government is not merely the activity of the state officials and institutions. For Waring, governance was a way of exercising power that touched people as individuals and as "the people" in a single reach.

The goal was to create civic pride, Colonel Waring argued, and if "nothing is gained to the city except in a negative way, at least the neutrality of thousands of children has been purchased and the streets are cleaner from the fact that so many are kept from making them dirty."[15] In other words, Waring sought to link each volunteer to the resolution of collective social problems (including the lack of municipal power to enforce the sanitary code). The league encouraged the people to carry out the purpose of government. For sanitation reform to succeed, according to a report in *Engineering News*, "every citizen would be an inspector."[16]

The league employed what I am calling a technology of citizenship: it sought to make good citizens out of poor and recent immigrants, to expand the limits and maximize the powers of city government by making the people self-governing. It was voluntary, but it practiced an art of coercion that made children at once subject to government and subjects of self-government. "This profession [sanitary engineering] is neither that of physician, nor engineer, nor educator, but smacks of all three. It levies autocratic powers, kin to those of ancient tyrants, but at the same time depends upon the sheerest democracy of information and co-operation to give its work effect."[17] To be sure, this social government took place largely outside *the* government in voluntary associations and special commissions, but it was expressly political.

For progressives such as Colonel Waring and J. A. Hobson, the object of "the new social profession" was life, its conditions and health, and its civic or political engagement. (Readers will recognize in the Juvenile Street Cleaning League the contours of Foucault's concept of "bio-power," which is elaborated in Chapters 1 and 2.) Colonel Waring saw political as well as commodity value in garbage: "Dickens' 'Golden Dustman' and the accounts of the rag-pickers of Paris have made us familiar with the fact that there is an available value in the ordinary *rejectamenta* of human life. We learn by the work of the dock Italian of New York that to regain this value is a matter of minute detail; it calls for the recovery of unconsidered trifles from a mass of valueless wastes, and the conversion of these into a saleable commodity."[18] Waring learned from scavengers and immigrants that recycling is profitable, but he sought to render that commodity value of political use to the municipal government of New York City. Government, to be effective, must concern itself and its citizens with "minute detail," "trifles,"

and "valueless waste," for the smallest things were the means of transforming waste into political capital. Waring devised a classically liberal and
democratic technology to get the people to police themselves so that the
street-cleaning commissioner did not have to. The city was cleaner and the
citizens more active and civically minded; all this without the government
being directly involved. Today garbage is still linked to government, but
the link is evermore indirect and minute.

Around 1989 the garbage bins in my neighborhood were locked. A
minor and local reform, it shaped my own understanding of how power
works and how the political is constituted. The story — a set of anecdotes
loosely based on my memories and some research on the history of garbage
reform — goes something like this:

Walking to the bus stop, I noticed that Dumpsters in my Minneapolis
neighborhood had new locks. Among the many consequences of the
lockup, the most significant, it seemed to me, was that people who survived
on Dumpster-diving — recyclers and homeless people — were now much
less free to live on their own terms. Those struggling to stay out of the arms
of the poverty industry now had no recourse but to steal their subsistence
or submit to case management in one or another shelter or social service
program. It seemed obvious to me that the space of freedom was shrinking,
that the very means of subsistence were being enclosed behind the bars of
criminal justice and "helping."

I began to search for the authority, official, reason, or interest behind
the Dumpster lockup. I intended to protest, to badger that authority, to try
to reverse the decision. In a manner of speaking, I took up the cause. Much
later, I figured out that the effect rather than the cause was, if not the whole
story, the more important part.

First, I asked the cashier at a local convenience store why the Dumpster
in the parking lot was locked. He said that the store was liable if anyone getting into the bin was injured or made sick from ingesting its contents. I
doubted that it was a question of that particular store's liability, because
many stores had locked up their bins at about the same time. Certainly
people do get sick and injured from the contents of garbage containers. In
his memoir about living homeless, Lars Eighner reports that Dumpster-
diving has serious drawbacks as a way of life, "including dysentery about
once a month."[19] For a store to be sued by the sick and injured, though, is
extremely unlikely. When I inquired why the other stores locked their
Dumpsters as well, the cashier shrugged; the conversation was over.

Later on, I asked a neighborhood activist about the lockup. She said that residents living near the parking lot where one Dumpster sat complained about the drunks who congregated there on weekends. The noise, the nuisance, and the occasional fights spilled over from the parking lot into nearby yards. (She assumed, and I accepted at the time, that it was the trash bin that attracted the drinkers, even though the store sold no alcohol. Later I found out that because residents are obliged to arrange with the city in advance — and pay for — the collection of large objects such as furniture and appliances, some would covertly drop off such items near commercial Dumpsters. Drinkers congregated in those spots, then, because there were accommodations, couches and chairs.) She also mentioned that residents were concerned about children's safety because they were attracted to Dumpsters for treasure hunts and sometimes used them as a hideaways.

Still, I couldn't believe that the neighborhood association had that kind of clout with local businesses. Even after a protracted fight, the association had failed to prevent a garbage incinerator from going up on the edge of that inner-city neighborhood. Lest it begin to sound as if I am inventing this remarkable confluence of events having to do with garbage (which I have only begun to list), all these things happened during the three years I lived on the south side of Minneapolis while attending graduate school. Only the chain of events is hypothesized from my memory.

Around this time I heard about a homeless man who was killed while sleeping in a downtown Dumpster; a garbage truck emptied him into its crusher. Also, I learned that Dumpster-diving college students were making maps of local bins with timetables for the freshest spoils. In response to the fad, a bagel shop and a pizza place near campus stopped putting out their trash at night before eventually locking their bins.[20]

Somewhat confounded by this time, I still had faith that I could find and confront the real cause of the lockup. I went back to the convenience store and asked for the owner who was not in. I spoke to a manager, who claimed that people were dumping their household garbage, as well as washing machines and old couches, in or near the Dumpster. Since the store paid for garbage pickup by weight, he explained, the lockup was a cost-saving measure. Although there were fines for illegal dumping, the manager claimed that no one enforced the rules.[21] Grocers' associations as well as neighborhood associations do attempt to police the system themselves in more or less organized ways.[22]

Thus, the manager's explanation was plausible, based as it was on the bottom line, and it fit within the broader context of garbage reform. Throughout many states garbage disposal became more expensive in the 1980's because of environmental concerns and privatization. Landfills were closed or restricted from accepting lawn waste and large objects. Municipal garbage contracts for residences and the imposition of fees for disposing of motor oil, tires, refrigerators, and the like made the efforts to regulate garbage more vigilant. Illegal dumping, privatization, health, safety and environmental concerns, liability — all these were plausible reasons for locking garbage containers in the 1980s. Yet I still wanted to know who was responsible for devising and enacting the solution.

For a number of reasons I doubted that the manager's explanation was the whole story. First, the local stores were not associated; moreover, it was not only convenience or grocery stores that locked their Dumpsters but also nonprofits, clinics, and schools. Second, the reason he gave was exclusively based upon his private interest, but the context in which his interests were defined was not of his own making. His self-interest was an effect, then, rather than a cause of the changes. Third, despite the privatization of garbage contracts and the changes in environmental laws, lots of different people articulated their interest in the lock up; they often gave answers that coincided with other broad changes in the 1980s, such as the rise in the number of homeless people and the imperative to take personal responsibility for recycling. So many people I spoke with had perfectly good reasons for the lock up, and so many claimed responsibility, that I began to doubt that there was any one cause, one doer behind the deed. Was there more to the story?

I continued looking. Officials of the company that owned and emptied the Dumpsters could (or would) not tell me who instituted the lockup or whether there was a law they were complying with. Calls to their insurance company and to the city got the run-around but never an answer to my question. I was none too persistent in this aspect of my search because bureaucrats and company officials were less than forthcoming over the phone and I had no appeal: I could not claim to represent a large group or hire an attorney to represent me; I didn't want to pose as a journalist. Approaching individuals in person was a more successful tactic.

At a nearby grocery chain store, I asked a manager about the lockup. He thought I was asking him about salvageable food and assured me that the chain did not throw away anything edible, but passed items beyond their prime to local food shelves and soup kitchens (and, someone told me later, to school lunch programs).[23] His store's garbage and recycling facilities were behind a fence, he assured me, not to keep people out but to keep the garbage in and prevent its littering the parking lot and surrounding neighborhood.

I asked several people who worked in or around food banks and soup kitchens about the lockup. Each of them assured me that there was no need for anyone to eat out of garbage bins because free food was available — if not all the time, at least often enough to get by. Kent Beittel, executive director of the Open Shelter in Ohio, claimed that Dumpster-diving for food was unnecessary. According to the *Columbus Dispatch*, he said that "because of the city's generous donations to food pantries and soup kitchens, 'it is impossible to starve in this town.'" He added, however, that the "real question is what is happening with our social-service agencies that causes people to run these kinds of health risks instead of using resources available through the system."[24] A very good question, which I take up in Chapter 1.

No one I spoke to in the helping industries was particularly concerned about the lockup, tending to see it as a public health matter rather than a question of freedom. One food bank administrator did express disgust at the locked bins and at corporate food retailers. She acknowledged that recycling and scavenging could be marginally profitable, but she could not answer why people might avoid soup kitchens and charities if they could. "They're afraid, schizophrenic, paranoid, abused," she offered, but not because of anything in particular that the charities were doing. She suggested that Ronald Reagan was the real culprit because he was responsible for deinstitutionalizing so many mentally ill people, leaving them to fend for themselves.

As a welfare rights activist at the time, working in coalition with other groups involved in antipoverty movements, I mistrusted most social service workers and "helping" professionals myself. I asked homeless and formerly homeless people I organized with, mainly but not exclusively from a group called Up & Out of Poverty Now, about the Dumpsters. The overwhelming response was that the lockup was a way for "them" or "the system" to control people. When asked to be more specific, most said, "capitalists," "Reagan," "rich people," or "the city," indicating that, like me, other activists tended to believe that the powers-that-be made things happen and that their power insulated them from being held accountable for their power. Power did double duty for us as a "real" or "actual" cause and as that which rendered itself invisible or unaccountable; power was, tautologically, both cause and effect.

When I asked these same people if they would like to take up the cause, they said that the Dumpster matter was small potatoes and not the "real" issue for homeless people or the impoverished. Again, there was a tautology at work. The "real" object of resistance was against those who had power, but because their power insulated them, it was the principal of power — rather than the powerful themselves or their specific actions — that was to be the object of resistance. In other words, acts of power and powerful actors are caused by power. (I discuss the tautological conception of power and the question of resistance at length in Chapters 1, 3, and 5.)

My confusion with all this competing and seemingly trivial information about Dumpsters turned to utter stupefaction when a short time later the city instituted a set of "incentives" for encouraging residential recycling. Households were to pay by the pound for garbage hauling, whereas recycling was to be free and curbside. Was there no end to reform, to new plans, fads and events, interests, and purposes surrounding the disposal of garbage? Was my own concern about freedom merely idiosyncratic? Was there no one in charge of or accountable for these reforms? No one voted on them; there was no general public discussion. So who was responsible?

I finally resolved to go with what I had. I sorted over all the different reasons that were given for the lockup which I had initially discounted because they were contradictory and seemed irrelevant to my goal of finding the doer of the deed. Strangely, all these interests-at-odds never clashed. Insurance companies, the city, garbage contractors, neighborhood activists, store owners, all found that their (different) interests were served by the lockup. Either most were seriously deluded, and only one or two coinciding interests were in fact served, or I was deluded in thinking that a particular set of interests had to be served for an act of power like the lockup to occur. No common interest was articulated, only particular and local interests, yet collective action was taken. Was some invisible hand at work? A happy coincidence for all but the excluded Dumpster-divers?

In short, I found that I had no cause. Compared with the search for Roger in Michael Moore's documentary film, *Roger and Me*, my search had no clear object but ended in similar frustration.[25] Whereas Roger was *somewhere* behind closed doors, waiting to be exposed like Oz for the coward that he was, perhaps the object of my search wasn't hidden away, but simply didn't exist apart from local folklore and the innumerable new plans, schemes, local and national trends affecting garbage. No law, no decree, no contracting parties had determined the outcome of locked Dumpsters. Worse yet, I realized I had no strategy for contesting an act of power if I could not find, let alone confront, the powerful.

The task for democratic theory, faced with the facelessness of power, could be understood as the effort to give power a face or a name, to make it visible and accountable. During the postwar period democratic theorists on the left did attempt to reveal the hidden countenance of power even, or especially, when the powerful did not visibly act on their interest. Invisible acts such as "nondecisions," "nonparticipation" or political apathy, and invisible truths such as "objective interests" (as opposed to manifest interests) were conceptualized to reveal the interests and powers that operated precisely by making themselves invisible and thereby subverting the otherwise inevitable conflict with those upon whom they acted. On the right, in that school of democratic theory named by the apparent oxymoron "democratic elitism," or "democratic pluralism," political scientists such as Robert Dahl pursued the assumption that where there was no overt conflict, no power could have been exercised. Without visible conflict, he argued, there was no act of power, no exclusion, no oppression. What was invisible was not an act of power or the interest of the powerful but the silent consent of unequal parties to their inequality and to the system of government more broadly.

In either case, democratic theory was driven by what was not there. Each party to what came to be known as the "three faces of power debate" explained that what was not visible was *really* there, either objective interests and latent resistance or an implicit consensus. Though not visible or intelligible, a face was surely lurking behind the shadow appearance of political apathy and inaction. Both sides assumed that a face-to-face confrontation with power was both a possibility and a measure of democratic freedom. This had been my assumption, too, until I took up the cause of Dumpster-diving.

Once I realized that my desire to act on the level of the macro-political — to confront the sovereign decision-makers — was thwarted by the micro-political, then the profusion of those small and confusing events, interests, and acts became the real story to tell. New questions arose. What makes it possible for so many contradictory interests to be served without clashing with one another? If acts of power are anonymous, how can we say they are still democratic? Why did so many different people articulate their responsibility and interests in such small things as locking up garbage? Why did I? In what sense are reforms — whether small changes with no grand structural impact or large changes of whole systems — with no clear causality, no clear line of authority, democratic? Absent an actual cause, in what sense can reforms be resisted?

Oddly enough, the League of Women Voters promised to answer my questions with the publication of a pamphlet, *The Garbage Primer*, in 1993.[26] In the name of citizen education and active participation, the primer sets out to educate citizens like me on the forms and tactics of participation for everyone with a stake in garbage reform (according to the primer, that includes just about everyone). The primer is limited, however, to concerns of the environment, disposal methods, hazardous waste, and cost. It does not answer the questions listed above or my concern for freedom but repeats Colonel Waring's faith that the citizen is sovereign and the most effective politically because each one carries the responsibility for how garbage is handled. To get the average citizen to act, the primer insists, all that is necessary is to provide information about the technical aspects of disposal, a list of alternative methods of disposal, and tips for getting involved in decision-making processes. Of course, the Socratic assumption that citizens fail to act only out of ignorance assumes that all those I talked to knew the same thing. In fact, they each knew what the real problem was, but in no sense could they have come to agree.

But the people I spoke to, with the possible exception of the neighborhood activist, *did* take responsibility for the garbage lockup without ever having involved themselves in public or political decision-making. In fact, the terrain I traveled in search of a cause was not "the political" in any traditional sense, nor were the interests involved necessarily those of organized interest groups. Yet everyone seemed to have an interest. I came to suspect that all the individuals who took responsibility for the lockup, though not engaged in a conspiracy, were the points of articulation for a kind of power I didn't understand and a form of politics I could see no way into.

The impetus for this book was a blindness that seeing clearly could not cure. Rather than another theory or an alternative vision of democracy and citizenship, I needed to understand the mode of government by which individuals take responsibility for small things.

That same impetus only grew stronger when I found myself in an activist's version of the welfare trap. For several years I was steeped in the inadequacies, petty humiliations, and crushing poverty of AFDC (Aid to Families with Dependent Children). As a welfare rights activist I was deeply opposed to AFDC because the sums of money meted out were so small that no one could live decently, let alone well, on welfare. As a system of power, welfare seemed designed to hold single mothers down. Then again, it was impossible to be *against* welfare because it was the only stable source of in-come and health benefits for so many women and children.

Proponents and critics of welfare have changed sides over the last ten years, but the possible positions on welfare have not changed.[27] It is a po-litical trap: I cannot be for or against welfare; there is no way to win. I hope to draw others into the same trap in order that we may think anew about welfare and social services and the ways they are tied to freedom, power, justice, and politics: that is, the ways in which small and contingent things connect up to the grand scheme of things.

The practices of welfare do not lend themselves to analytical precision. If a juvenile court official orders a mother to graduate from a self-esteem program because she failed to protect or to discipline her child (a program operated, say, by an explicitly feminist organization combatting domestic violence), is that act political, judicial, or administrative? If Wisconsin docks a family's welfare check for a child's truancy, a program called "learn-fare," what kind of punishment or justice is it? Social, civil, familial? If a private, nonprofit organization incarcerates an allegedly drug-addicted pregnant woman, is it usurping the jurisdiction of the courts, or is it creat-ing a new political jurisdiction?

To take up any of these questions as a cause, whether the garbage lockup or the protection of poor women from overly zealous "help," means an endless search for a sovereign power that is not there. To take up these questions as effects of the changing configuration of the political, however, would be to refigure the territory of politics itself rather than to wrestle the causes.

At first, I sought to politicize the Dumpster lockup by holding whoever caused it politically accountable. That is, I sought to bring the issue into the political realm of contestation, thus leaving the structure of the political as it was, yet adding to it. Even if every small thing is political, they cannot *all* be drawn into the political. As William Connolly points out, words and things are not essentially contested but contingently contested.[28] Nor is it the case that if every little thing is political, politics is everywhere — even if power may be. What is required of democratic theory is less a solution to the conundrum of the political than a way to articulate the contingency of the political that neither exhausts nor determines any efforts to reconsti-tute political order and the space of politics.

Although my themes are large and include an examination of the bound-aries between subjectivity and subjection, democracy and despotism, social intervention and the limited liberal state, the social and the political, welfare and citizenship, I trace those boundaries through the minute practices of self-government in the history of democratic and social reform. I analyze each of these boundaries more in terms of its details than as philosophical questions of difference in nature or meaning. Instead of saying what democracy — or any of the boundaries just listed — should be, I attempt to explain how it is done, how it is thought and practiced.

Again, rather than envisioning democracy differently, my goal is to undermine the self-evidence of the notion that democracy is a good thing, pure and simple, the best form of government; the assumption that we all know what it is; the conviction that democratic forms of government are more free than any other form. Democratic relations are still relations of power and as such are continually recreated, which requires that democratic theory never presuppose its subject but persistently inquire into the constitution of that subject.

1

Democratic Subjects

> However, if you take power and independence from a municipality, you
> may have docile subjects but you will not have citizens.
>
> ALEXIS DE TOCQUEVILLE

At least since Tocqueville drew his famous contrast between citizens and subjects in the 1830s, it has served as a critical measuring stick, albeit a contested one, for distinguishing the activities and qualities of democratic citizenship from other modes of political action.[1] To be subject to the power or authority of another is taken to be the antithesis of democratic citizenship. Tocqueville held that self-governing citizens have the capacity and the power to participate in politics, to act on their collective interests, desires, and goals. Whereas subjects behave themselves because an external force exerts power over them, citizens have the power to act for themselves; they are their own masters.

After a brief caveat on the title, "democratic subjects," this chapter explains why it is misleading to separate the terms of subjectivity, agency, and citizenship from those of subjection, domination, and powerlessness in democratic theory. Against the grain of democratic theory, I argue that the democratic citizen is not a species apart from the subject, from the welfare recipient, the bureaucratic client, the exploited worker, or the therapeutic patient. Being "just another number," "dependent," or "in need of help" is not the antithesis of being an active citizen. Rather, it is to be in a tangled field of power and knowledge that both enables and constrains the possibilities of citizenship.

My argument that citizens and subjects are not opposites, that citizens are made and therefore subject to power even as they become citizens, is not intended to undermine democratic theory. I understand democratic theory as a constitutive discourse that helps to solidify what it is possible to think, do, say, be, and feel as a citizen. Recognizing that democratic theory is a constitutive discourse means also attending to the ways in which it is constitutive of any attempt to change it. The contrast between citizens and subjects will continue to shape democratic discourses, even those such as my own that are critical of the contrast. For instance, I do not read against Tocqueville. I am reading *Democracy in America* as it is usually read, as an exemplary text of democratic theory.

First, I examine several of the subjects that drive contemporary democratic theory: citizenship, political apathy, and powerlessness; another, the social, is examined in the next chapter. I find that radical democrats and pluralists alike reproduce the citizen/subject dichotomy and so continue to obscure the ways in which citizens are made. As a case in point, I show how that dichotomy works to undermine the radically democratic objectives of small "d" democrats such as Sheldon Wolin. Second, I rehearse the "three faces of power" debate in political science and situate the problems that shaped normative democratic theory into a positive science of citizenship, giving concrete expression to the will to empower. The operationalization of democratic theories of power are linked here and in Chapter 3 to technologies of citizenship. Third, I link the operationalization of social scientific knowledge to what Theresa Funiciello calls "the professionalization of being human" or what Foucualt called "bio-power." Using welfare reform, I illustrate what I mean by the claim that citizens are made.

Subjects

A caveat: I will not, for the sake of consistency, fix the meanings of the terms "subject" and "subjectivity" in advance for the reader. Analytical precision is neither possible nor desirable at the moment; I have neither the desire nor the ability to bring an end to what has been an enormously productive, if seriously destabilizing, case of what Ludwig Wittgenstein called "conceptual puzzlement."[2] In this predicament, one cannot say what a word means apart from how it is used, or what it is used to say.[3]

Such uses might productively confound meaning, for example, when a single word is uttered to say two things at once. Foucault used the word "subject" in a double sense, not to confuse things with doubletalk but to articulate a form of power that simultaneously "subjugates and makes subject to."[4] That is, he means to say that modern forms of power tie the subjectivity (conscience, identity, self-knowledge) of the individual to that individual's subjection (control by another). The subject is one who is both under the authority of another and the author of her or his own actions. Foucault means to undermine the perspective from which power can be perceived only as the antithesis of freedom, a perspective from which it would be possible to recognize Foucault's claim only as a contradiction or a paradox. In other words, he uses the term to change what it is possible to say.

According to Wittgenstein, to change what it is possible to say is also to change what it is possible to do, to think, or to be. From that perspective, the varied uses of "subject" and "subjectivity" are expressions of the struggle to define ourselves. For example, "subject" and "subjectivity" have undergone a rigorous interrogation in feminist theory. At stake is the possibility of living life differently as a woman, or for women perhaps to live not as "women" but as subjects capable of constituting their own gender. By and in the large, debates over the subject in feminist and poststructural theory are over questions of strategy and the possibilities for resistance. Like poststructural feminists, Foucault hoped to "promote new forms of subjectivity" in part by changing what it is possible to say. To insist on a definition of "subject" or "woman" at this juncture would be to close down the possibility of becoming a new kind of subject.

To avoid confusion, then, insofar as that is possible concerning a word with many and varied usages, I offer the following list of the senses to which I put the word "subject"—though no entry is entirely exclusive of any other.

First, in the terms laid out by Tocqueville, a subject is "one who is subject to the power and authority of a another," usually a sovereign power such as a king, a majority, or the law. To be subject, in other words, is to be subjugated, to be powerless, passive, the opposite of a democratic citizen. This meaning of "subject" survives in social scientific uses of "power" as the possession of one party over and above another. On this view, the world can be divided into citizens and subjects, those who have power and those who do not. These senses of both "subject" and "power" are endemic to the "three faces of power" debate in democratic theory, which is treated further on. For the moment, it is enough to emphasize that here the "subject" is defined against the "citizen."

Second, in the title of this chapter, "democratic subjects" is meant to indicate the subject matter of democratic theory, all that is deemed appropriate to the field of inquiry traversed by democratic theorists and all that is deemed relevant to the study of democracy. This sense of "subject" is confounded by the fact that we also refer to the subject matter of any discipline as "objects of inquiry," or things that are perceptible. "Democratic subjects" is also meant to signify that democracy is a form of government that requires a new kind of subject rather than a form of government that liberates the subject from under the sovereign.

The third sense of "subject," related to the second, also contravenes "object." Today we might refer to Tocqueville's subject as an "object" of power.[5] A subject, after Kant, has possession of him- or herself and is no longer the object of another's will or knowledge but now the subject of consciousness and self-motivation. In this modern sense, the subject is one in possession of the power to command oneself, a "subject of power" rather than a mere "object of power." The "subject" in this sense is often used as a synonym for "individual," "knower," "agent," or "actor."

Fourth, I use "citizen-subject" to hold together the first and the third usages but not to conflate them. "Citizen-subject" is not used here to indicate a contradiction or a dichotomy but to indicate that although democratic citizens are formally free, their freedom is a condition of the operationalization of power. In the third sense as developed by Marx, the subject is the source of desire and is a subject only so long as that desire is a product of his or her own consciousness. To say that any persons are no longer subjects is to say that their consciousness, and so their desire, has been altered or fabricated in some way. For Marx, the first sense of "subject" is the antithesis of the third.

Finally, I use the hyphenated "citizen-subject" to indicate that neither the first nor the third sense of "subject" is the antithesis of the other. Neither can stand for an ontological being. My concern is to focus attention on the mutually constitutive relations between these two senses of "subject." To see the citizen-subject in this way is potentially to reconfigure ways of being and thinking about citizens, of acting politically and governing ourselves.

Again, it is my hope that if I critically articulate the structure of democratic discourse, citizens and subjects will no longer appear to be the only political creatures inhabiting the world of democracy. The normative definitions of citizen/subject are, variously and in deeply contested ways, insinuated within the critical vocabularies of postwar political struggles: participation versus exclusion, equality versus difference, ideology versus reality, the political versus the social, freedom versus domination, power versus powerlessness, autonomy versus dependency, public versus private, among others. Each of these binaries separates the terms of agency and freedom from the terms of repression and domination, the terms of subjectivity from the terms of subjection.

Of course, the binary citizen/subject is not set in stone. It is unstable, contested, and inseparable from what Eve Sedgwick describes as "the context of an entire cultural network of normative definitions, definitions themselves equally unstable but responding to different sets of contingencies and often at a different rate."[6] I am most interested in how "citizen/subject" is embedded within the terms of welfare and social reform.

In Tocqueville's understanding, the citizen has the autonomy and the power to act; the subject does not. Although power is available for use by the citizen, Tocqueville does not understand it to be a property of the citizen per se. If the possession and use of power is what determines the difference between citizens and subjects, however, then power is not external to but constitutive of their difference.

In short, I am suggesting that if power is not external to the state of being citizen or subject, if to be self-governing is to be both citizen and subject, both subject to and the subject of government, then a welfare recipient, for example, is not the antithesis of an active citizen. She will undoubtedly be the subject of bureaucratic control but will also have plenty of opportunities to resist — individually and collectively — the definitions and regulations imposed upon her. It is significant that welfare and most social programs are voluntary. Even when they are overtly coercive, they work by getting the recipient to see her own interests in those control strategies. Discourse structures a field of possible actions rather than determined outcomes. She is, then, both the subject of and subject to welfare discourses, not merely their object.

It is to indicate that citizens are both subjected to power and subjects in their own right that I replace the dichotomizing slash in citizen/subject with a hyphen: citizen-subject. Of course, it would be in vain to suggest that replacing a slash with a hyphen actually confers upon subjects a place in the politics of citizenship. Discourse works by telling us in advance of any perception what it is we can see and what is or is not important.[7] Discourse continues its work even after its structure is recognized (for example, even after it is recognized that heterosexuals are a recent invention of scientific and popular discourses, the difference between hetero- and homosexuals does not disappear).[8] Still, by incorporating citizen-subjects into democratic discourse, I hope to promote a political awareness of how citizen-subjects are made.

Citizens and Subjects

When citizenship is measured in this way, citizen against subject, it is almost impossible for the mass of citizens not to fall short. Paradoxically, the demos cannot measure up to the standard of autonomous citizenship and self-definition if the very definition of being citizens is set in advance of their engagement in politics. As a critical measure, citizen/subject separates the state of subjection from that of autonomous agency. But it does so only by presuming in advance of any analysis that the categories of measurement are self-evident, that there are in fact two distinct kinds of individuals: the citizen and the subject.[9]

The ways that citizens are rendered as subjects of democratic discourse has critical implications for democratic politics. When we say today that someone is subject, acquiescent, dependent, or apathetic, we are measuring that person against a normative ideal of citizenship.[10] As a result, the discourses of democratic citizenship tend to foreclose the ways in which it is possible to be a citizen rather than seeking to place the question of citizenship within the reach of ordinary citizens.[11]

What is most important, undergirding the contests about what citizenship means, is that the self-evidence of critical categories such as citizen/subject makes it unnecessary to inquire into *how* power works to make subjects out of citizens and citizens out of subjects. If we fail to scrutinize the ways that citizens are made, we may completely overlook the constitutive discourses of citizenship that are characteristic of liberal democracies.

For example, in "What Revolutionary Action Means Today," an essay first published in 1982, Sheldon Wolin objects to the silence he hears on the subject of citizenship: "While there are many voices, with varying degrees of good faith, ready to testify for democracy . . . there is virtually no one who is given to reflecting about the democratic citizen, to asking what it is to be one, or why, if each of us is one and there are so many of us, the society seems to have so many anti-democratic tendencies."[12] The "significant silence" that Wolin hears is to my ears a veritable roar. As I document throughout this book, it seems that everybody has a scheme, a social program, an organizing strategy, or an issue campaign for turning political subjects into democratic citizens, for transforming the apathetic into the politically active, the indolent into the productive, and the dependent into the self-sufficient (recall Colonel Waring's scheme from the introduction).

There are, in fact, innumerable programs and strategies devised by social reformers, feminists, neighborhood activists, policymakers and legislators, entrepreneurs and social scientists, all in a state of seemingly perpetual reform. Sometimes such fabrications are obvious, such as when the Freedmen's Bureau sought to make citizens out of former slaves, "enterprise zones" to make entrepreneurs who would improve the economies and reduce crime in poor neighborhoods, and the Community Action Programs (studied in Chapter 3) to promote "maximum feasible participation." Even when such programs fail, the strategies they invent are re-formed and continue to shape efforts to make citizens. More often, strategies for making citizens are subtle or not expressly "political," such as the accounting methods in large welfare bureaucracies (examined in Chapter 5) and the self-esteem movement (Chapter 4).

In order to hear the abundance of discourse on citizenship, however, Wolin would have to alter several of the presumptions that drive his radically democratic criticism of the liberal order. I focus on Wolin's arguments here in part because his influence on the radical democratic tradition is so profound.[13] Understanding itself as an antiliberal alternative to state socialism, one strand of radical democracy has taken a pluralist turn away from the kinds of presumptions that I am interrogating in Wolin's work.[14] His presumptions about citizenship, however, are representative of those that continue to shape democratic discourse in general; in particular, they shape the rationalities of neoliberal and neoconservative reform efforts, from empowerment zones and workfare to volunteerism.

First, according to Wolin, a citizen who is recognizably constructed is by definition no longer an authentically democratic citizen but a bureaucratic subject or merely a bearer of a prepolitical interests or identity: "Interest group politics dissolves the idea of the citizen as one for whom it is natural to join together with other citizens to act for purposes related to a general community and substitutes the idea of individuals who are grouped according to conflicting interests. . . . He or she is instead [of a citizen] a business executive, a teamster, a feminist, office worker, farmer, or homosexual whose immediate identity naturally divides him or her from others."[15]

Wolin uses the citizen/subject antithesis as a critical wedge into the antidemocratic forces of modernity, including the modes of resistance adopted by social movements. For Wolin, if we choose to differentiate ourselves as particular kinds of citizens — feminist, union member, Chicano, black, welfare recipient, or queer — rather than as citizens of the polity, we are no longer bearers of a properly political identity. He takes human differences of race, gender, and class to be prepolitical, yet social movements since the 1960s were organized on the principle of politicizing those categories. If human differences were not natural but constructed, social movements argued, it was possible to change them through political means.

Against the politicizations of power in sexual, familial, educational, racial, and economic relations which characterized new social movements, Wolin argues that those who were politically engaged in resistance in the 1960s and 1970s were acting in the capacity of "depoliticized" subjects.[16] Wolin calls those who engaged in new social movements "groupies": "The citizen, unlike the groupie, has to acquire a perspective of commonality, to think integrally and comprehensively rather than exclusively. The groupie never gets beyond 'politics,' the stage of unreflective self interest."[17] Caught up in politics, then, the groupie cannot join citizens in collective efforts confined in the "the political." Perhaps another way to say this is that Wolin's proper citizens do not choose their own conceptions of themselves as citizens or act to transform the boundaries of the political.[18] Both those boundaries and the standard of democratic citizenship are fixed prior to the political action of citizens.[19]

Why does a committed democratic theorist so sharply chastise those who demand to participate in setting the terms of their own citizenship? Wolin insists that any political action that does not conform to a communal standard of democratic citizenship is "depoliticized." For example, he holds that the grassroots movements flourishing in the Reagan years were "politically incomplete. There are major problems in our society that are general in nature and necessitate modes of vision and action that are comprehensive rather than parochial."[20] Social movements and grassroots politics were merely prerequisites to real and authentic democratic action aimed at the state. "These developments are suggestive because they represent the first steps ever toward systematic popular intervention in the sacrosanct domain of state secrets and national security. This [the state] is new terrain for democratic politics and it is genuinely political."[21] Somehow, both the actions and the inactions of citizens provide Wolin with evidence for the claim that we are "depoliticized."

Wolin revised his argument somewhat in the mid-1980s, suggesting that through grassroots activism "the political can become incorporated in the everyday lives of countless people."[22] Nevertheless, by referring back to a premodern standard of the political in order to comprehend the present, he rules out the possibilities for a democratic politics in the present: "It is clearly impossible to impose a democratic conception of the citizen upon the political realities of the megastate. . . . The democratic conception of the citizen must be preserved as an ideal form, the measuring rod of what it means to be a citizen."[23] Yet, to measure citizens against that standard is to negate the possibility of being or becoming democratic citizens in the present, a conclusion confirming his initial claim that there is silence on the subject of citizenship.

In Wolin's lexicon, both the ideal of democracy and "the political" are critical standards against which he measures all eventualities.[24] But they are one and the same standard, since he uses the two ideal concepts synony-mously: "Democracy stands for an alternative conception of politics, even a standing criticism of and a living opposition to the megastate and media politics."[25] If politics, conflict, and action are not "genuinely democratic"— that is, communal — they are by definition depoliticized, antipolitical, or prepolitical. It is not possible that the borders of the political might be set democratically because they define that which is democratic or not, politi-cal or not. By reducing "the political" to a particular form of democracy that we do not practice, Wolin abandons us to the megastate.

If political action cannot aim at differentiating citizens from one an-other or at reconstituting the political, then there is no reason to inquire into how democratic government works. In its ideal form, Wolin argues, the relationship between citizen and democratic polity is entirely transpar-ent. In a truly democratic polity there is no need to fashion democratic modes of governance. All that is necessary is for democratic theory to sweepingly dismiss the megastate and hold out for an ideal alternative. (Wolin defies his own conclusions in his later examination of governmen-tal practices in welfare states.)[26]

In the sweep of Wolin's critical definitions, most of the forms of mod-ern government that are constitutive of citizenship gather under the head-ings of "the social" and "the depoliticized." He writes, for example, "there are, of course, many reasons for the political passivity of the unemployed and the permanently poor, but one of the most important is the depoliticization to which they have been subjected."[27] Wolin is arguing that depoliticization is both a cause and an effect of political passivity. When we do not act politically, we are subject to a kind of power that operates to mask its own exercise. According to Wolin, if citizens do not participate in politics, the task of a critical democratic theory is to investigate how their natures have been tampered with, to uncover the powers that have "depoliticized" the naturally political citizen. The critical standard of "the genuinely political" effectively reduces the subject matter appropriate to democratic theory to the judgment of this or that according to the critical standards of citizenship and the political.

To back up his claim that citizenship is "depoliticized," Wolin follows Hannah Arendt in suggesting that the premodern political is replaced in modernity by the social. "Depoliticization is more extreme among the poor and racial minorities because they are the most helpless of all groups in the political economy, the new social form that is replacing the older form of the political order."[28] Under these same circumstances, social movements contested what was to count as politics (as in "the personal is political"). In contrast, Wolin's presumption is that the "genuinely political" is timeless. The politics of feminists and others, including "politics" in the sense of conflict of interest, the exercise of rights, the struggle for power, social movements, and protest, are not properly political. The question Wolin asks — what is "genuinely" political and what is not? — is as misguided as Robert Dahl's question: "Who governs?" (treated below).

[Democratic theory, with important exceptions, counts voting and open rebellion as "political" actions, for example, but neglects or dismisses the constitution of citizens in the therapeutic, disciplinary, programmatic, institutional, and associational activites of everyday life. Dismissing these activities and their locations as administrative, social, "prepolitical" or "depoliticizing" reduces democratic criticism to documenting the exclusion of certain subjects from the homogeneous sphere of the political, from the places and powers of citizenship.]

Homo Politicus and Homo Civicus:
Democracy and Power

The juxtaposition of citizen and subject is consistent with a way of thinking about power that was common to theories of pluralist democracy in the post-World War II period.[29] The political problematic driving those debates concerned the rise of the civil rights and other social movements and the mounting sociological evidence that liberal democratic regimes produced economic, social, racial, and political inequality. Does the presence of inequality signify that capitalist liberal democracies (measured against socialism during the Cold War) are not the best possible system of government? If we are formally equal in the eyes of the law, at the ballot box, and as parties to a contract, why does inequality persist? If the people do not have the power, who does? These questions shaped a debate over power that was never resolved, despite which, I discover in them the constitutive aspects of democratic discourse.

Democratic theorists sought to make the persistence of inequality intelligible by problematizing democracy in terms of the lack of political participation and powerlessness. In the process, as I argue in Chapter 3, the ideological debates over power rendered the lack of power and participation amenable to governmental intervention. The ideological debates between liberal and Marxist social scientists were transformed into a positive science of politics for knowing and intervening in reality, for operationalizing the various theories of power. What emerged out of those debates was not any agreement on the truth about power but a positive discourse of power, a method for contesting power in the shape of what was not there, a method for ordering and intervening in what had no prior existence.

For the moment, let me rehearse the debates over power in order to show that they exhibit a will to empower, a will to represent and speak for the interests of others. The most influential pluralist in the immediate postwar era was Robert Dahl. He posed the question, "Who governs?" (As I point out below, much the same question guided critics of pluralism, C. Wright Mills in particular, to answer, "The power elite.")

Pluralism — or as it was also called, "empirical democratic theory" and "democratic elitism"— claimed that the relative absence of political conflict in the United States, despite blatant and visible inequalities, signaled the deliberate if inarticulate consent of people who *chose* not to act politically. Pluralists claimed that direct political participation was not an essential or desirable feature of democracy. Consider Dahl's famous dismissal of the "classical" view: "It would clear the air of a good deal of cant if instead of assuming that politics is a normal and natural concern of human beings, one were to make the contrary assumption that whatever lip service citizens pay to conventional attitudes, politics is a remote, alien, and unrewarding activity."[30] The logic of pluralism indicated that if the mass of people did not participate directly in democratic political life it was because, as rational actors, citizens could achieve what they wanted through economic and private activity and had little time for or interest in politics.

In *Who Governs? Democracy and Power in an American City*, a study of New Haven, Dahl distinguished between the natures of *homo politicus*, the citizen actively engaged in governmental processes, and *homo civicus*, whose identities and interests are shaped and met in the ungoverned and nonpolitical realm of civil society.[31] *Homo civicus* designated the vast majority of potential voters, who rarely pursued their interests by engaging in politics. *Homo politicus* — the elected representative, interest-group advocate, and policy activist — actively participated in the process of government (narrowing the definition of political action to the electoral arena). At the same time Dahl argued that the political process is a completely open one. Since in his line of vision there were no persons or groups clamoring to engage at the level of government, he concluded that no citizens in New Haven were being excluded from participating. Significantly, less than six years after *Who Governs?* was published in 1961, clashes between the police force and black residents of New Haven made state violence daily news.[32]

Radical democrats such as Sheldon Wolin and the New Left generally despised the pluralist assumption that "man is by nature an a-political animal." To them, American pluralism seemed a thinly veiled apology for the inequality and elitism that characterized American politics. Critics of pluralism sought to disclose the invisible operation of power that excluded the masses from participation (for example, the media manipulation of mass interpretations; the bureaucratic domination that pervaded and depoliticized political and economic inequality; control of the state by economic elites). Democratic critics generally took political participation to be an essential feature of democracy; nonparticipation revealed that power was in the hands of elites and that the political participation of the masses was repressed or controlled. If people did not rebel against their oppression and political exclusion, then there must be some invisible coercion or threat hidden behind their acquiescence. That was, of course, power. What lurked in the shadow of *homo civicus* was power, not consent. Radical democrats believed that to reveal the truth of power, to assign it a face, would be to transform quiescence into a confrontation.

For example, in *Regulating the Poor*, Frances Fox Piven and Richard Cloward explained that welfare provision in the modern state was a response to the political rebellion of the destitute during periods of contraction in the capitalist economy and a mode of regulating labor in times of political quietude. During periods of mass unrest the expansion of welfare provision aimed at restoring political order not by "buying off" the poor but by bolstering the social control mechanisms of the market. "The trigger that sets off disorder is not economic distress itself, but the deterioration of social control. To restore order, the society must create the means to reassert its authority. Because the market is unable to control men's behavior, at least for a time, a surrogate system of social control must be evolved, at least for a time."[33] For Piven and Cloward, welfare was a system of social control for maintaining political and economic order.[34] Once such social control mechanisms succeeded in restoring order, the function of welfare turned to regulating labor by enforcing low-wage work.

Welfare, then, was an expression of capitalist class interests. The exclusion of the masses from participation was one effect of the organization of those interests in the state. Against the pluralist thesis that the political process is an open one, Piven and Cloward argued that even those modes of participation available to the masses — the vote and protest — were "delimited by the social structure." That is, the class structure of capitalism ensured that poor people's political organizations could not effectively challenge that structure.[35] Following Marx, Piven and Cloward argued that formal political equality was little more than a liberal myth that masked the real workings of power.[36] They challenged the pluralist thesis that the inarticulate consent of the masses accounted for their lack of participation. What appeared to be consent, they argued, was in fact a festering discontent held back only by the invisible operation of power. The race riots of the 1960s and scattered throughout the 1970s marked those moments when social control was weak.

The social control thesis is that power works coercively and secretly to *prevent* resistance and rebellion. The pluralist thesis is that consent is the secret behind the failure of the mass of citizens to rebel. Despite their ideological differences, theorists of democracy on the left and the right shared a basic conceptualization of power. As Steven Lukes wrote, summarizing the debates among proponents of the elitist, reformist, and radical theories of power: "The three views we have been considering can be seen as alternative interpretations and applications of one and the same underlying concept of power, according to which A exercises power over B when A affects B in a manner contrary to B's interests."[37] Their common object of analysis was to locate power by identifying instances in which A's interests were served and B's were not — or to prove that there were no such instances. The expectation behind the formulaic hypotheses of each "face" of power was the possibility of proving or disproving the truth of power: either some people were excluded from power and from the pursuit of happiness (according to the first and second faces), or they were quite happy and therefore apathetic about being unequal, (according to the third).

Each "face" assumed that power can be rationally and intentionally used by someone to affect (influence) other people. In other words, power is exercised unitarily, not as a struggle or in the relations between two or more parties, but in the causal effect of one upon another. Radical theorists sought to locate power after the fact, when B failed to protest against the power of A over conditions of inequality. Reformists asked whether agendas were set in advance in such a way that conflicts were diverted from erupting by the "mobilization of bias." Why look before and after the fact? Because the concern was with the lack of political participation: the problem was to explain what was not there. "Latent" dissent, "nondecisions," and "nonparticipation" on the part of the powerless were taken on the left as (invisible) signs of the domination that led to the "decision" not to participate.[38] Another way to say this is that citizens may or may not take a certain action: if they do so as a matter of their own interest, no power is involved; if they do so against their interest, then power is present and they act not as citizens but as the subjects of another.

In any case, there was general agreement that power could not be voluntary and coercive at the same time.[39] An action taken could not be an effect (caused by or taken under the influence) of power if it was voluntary. Lukes ruled out the possibility that B's real interests or desires could be shaped by power and still belong to B. If B voluntarily acts one way rather than another then no power is present, since power is considered only as an external and repressive force before or after the fact with no constitutive role in action. The possibility that power might be a positive force revealed in action is ruled out.

Lukes came very close to admitting that an action could be voluntary and coerced at the same time when he suggested that desire could be a product of power: "The radical, however, maintains that men's wants may themselves be a product of a system which works against their intersts, and, in such cases, relates the latter to what they would want and prefer, were they able to make the choice."[40] Lukes's neo-Marxist or Gramscian view of power depends upon the a priori counterfactual of "real" or "objective" interests to explain what does not happen, conflicts that do not erupt, and the possibility that people can be wrong about their own interests. To be "objective," however, desires must have their origin in the actor, never in power. Desires that are the products of power, Lukes held, should be seen not as material consequences of the exercise of power or a part of reality but as ideological falsehoods superimposed upon reality.

By ruling out the possibility that power relations could be simultaneously voluntary and coercive, that one's desire could be both one's own and a product of power, Lukes implied that the only authentically democratic polity would be one in which there are no relations of rule — one could be only self-ruling but never ruled in turn. Like Wolin, Lukes argued that the condition of freedom is the complete transparency of power relations. The critical evaluation of power relationships and inequality rested on the imagination of a democratic politics without power and a political subjectivity untouched by it. In addition to ruling out the possibility that real desires and interests may be shaped by power, Lukes dismissed the possibility that one could take real pleasure or have something to gain in submitting to power. His strategy was to give power a "face," to give B a face to replace the anonymous A, in order to hold the powerful accountable. (Recall the failure of my own attempt to do the same in the case of the dumpster lockup).

Holding B responsible for inaction was beside the point. B, in his or her innocence of power, was purely its object. The point was to transform B into a participatory, democratic actor.[41] The lack of political resistance was posed as a problem to be solved by producing the truth of power. Presumably, armed with the truth, the apathetic would realize the need for action to depose the powerful. For example, we ask why a battered woman does not leave the batterer, or why relatively few recipients, during the dismantling of the welfare state, organized any resistance? Faith in the truth of power — that is, that if only people knew the facts and ignored the newspapers, they would act — also shaped our expectations of democratic and feminist scholarship (which the debates over poststructuralism have amply illustrated).[42] The truth of power was never revealed in the "three faces" debate. Why does this way of posing the question of power persist, given how long the answer has been deferred and how long the face-to-face confrontation with power has been deferred? What can account for the persistent questioning of power in terms of the truth or falsity of domination and political exclusion?

Though I cannot answer these questions in full, I want to point out that both pluralists and radical theorists of democracy sought to represent those who did not speak out on their own behalf. In both cases, the truth of power was intended to speak in the voice of those who did not represent themselves. The will to speak the truth of power was in effect the will to speak on behalf of those whose silence placed a strain upon the legitimacy of liberal democratic government. (Of course, it is impossible to speak in the voice of the voiceless without first constituting their inability to speak for themselves.)

Further, both sides accepted that the measure of democratic freedom is the transparency of power and the openness of political processes.[43] If pluralists argued that power was transparent in the present despite inequality, then the left argued that invisible powers prevented the promise of openness from being realized. On all sides, "power" admitted into political analysis was seen to operate through the repression of the essential subjectivity of citizens and to result in their exclusion. So long as the transparency of power was accepted as the measure of democratic freedom, the question of how power actually works was displaced.

If we are to understand how democratic modes of government work, it is essential to ask not who has power and who does not, but how does power operate? If power relationships cannot be made wholly transparent, how can they be made democratic?

Producing the Poor, or Making Subjects

To understand how welfare provision contributes to the making of citizens, one must first refute the (currently) common wisdom that the welfare state is a system of social control, that the state *literally* produces the poor. Two recent books, one from the left and one from the right, suggest that a welfare system produces dependents (subjects) rather than citizens. Both books advance arguments that tie the subordination of welfare recipients to the powers and interests of elites. Each proposes the dismantling of the welfare state as a solution to poverty and the subjugation of poor people. A brief review of these proposals will show how commonplace understandings about the social construction of welfare recipients have become. Whereas both books, from opposed ideological perspectives, advance the thesis that the powers and interests of elites cause the subjection of poor people, I argue that neither explains why so many welfare recipients comply with a system that works against their own interests because the authors of the books mistake the production of subjectivity for its repression.

In *Losing Ground*, a book famously held to account for the welfare cuts made during the Reagan administration, Charles Murray argues that the Great Society programs "produced more poor."[44] Murray asserts that social

policies in the 1960s actually brought about the dependence of the poor and solidified the impoverished into a permanent class of dependents. Those results were inadvertent, he believes, and the Great Society's attempt to eradicate poverty was noble, if tragically wrongheaded and elitist. When policy-making elites responded to the civil rights movement with an expanded welfare system, according to Murray, their interests were not in improving the lives of blacks but in remedying their own white guilt. Through aiming to end poverty, social policy in fact developed a paternalistic system governed by liberal whites that encouraged the dependence of blacks. In short, the newly expanded welfare system did not end poverty but produced more poor people: "Theoretically, any program that mounts an intervention with sufficient rewards to sustain participation and an effective result will generate so much of the unwanted behavior (in order to become eligible for the program's rewards) that the net effect will be to increase the incidence of the unwanted behavior."[45]

In Murray's argument the problem boils down to the fact that liberal democratic programs are voluntary and so cannot demand or force their clients to make the sacrifices necessary to better their condition. So long as the success of programmatic aims is dependent upon people's voluntary participation, the program will be unable to demand that recipients do whatever is necessary to become self-sufficient. Following from his computation of the carrots and sticks delivered by the system of welfare, Murray advocates the complete dismantling of the welfare system in order to allow the market to determine and coerce the desired behavior.

Democratic government cannot force people to become self-sufficient, but, according to Murray, the market can. For example, "the technology of changing human behavior depends heavily on the use of negative reinforcement in conjunction with positive reinforcement."[46] In other words, motivations are always the same (self-interest), but behavior in pursuit of those interests is changeable. Behavior, then, can be determined by the organization of the social and structural order of incentives and disincentives. But only a free market structure can actually promote self-sufficiency. Murray's conception of social construction is remarkable for its determinism.

Despite its influence, Murray's book did not inaugurate the complete dismantling of welfare. Although AFDC is now all but dismantled, recipients have not been turned directly out into the cold of the market but turned over to a new system of perpetual job training. Still, Murray does not really answer why recipients complied with a system that produced their poverty. If all behavior is self-interested, why wouldn't rational people *choose* to subject themselves to the dictates of the market? His attempted answer is that welfare produced irrational behavior by overriding market incentives, especially among young black males. The labor market did not disappear, however, and if human beings are rationally self-interested, as Murray maintains, then they would choose to discipline themselves in the market rather than in the system of welfare. (Of course, Murray followed up *Losing Ground* with a book that undermined his own claim that all behavior is rational; in *The Bell Curve*, he argued that black male poverty is related to low IQ!)[47]

From the left, in *The Tyranny of Kindness*, Theresa Funiciello makes a different argument for dismantling the welfare system, but one that has the same basic structure as Murray's. According to her detailed and carefully documented indictment of the poverty industry, welfare works to create punitive, discretionary, and stigmatizing bureaucratic structures. More important, welfare works to enrich middle-class social service providers, corporations, and nonprofit foundations. Funiciello identifies the causes of poverty and the political exclusion of poor women, first, in the economic interests of the rich and of service providers and, second, in their ability to mask their prejudices and their economic interests in the ideology of helping. The bulk of most welfare budgets, she argues — including philanthropic, for-profit, state, county, and federal expenditures — goes into the pockets of the middle-class service providers, leaving poor women poor.

Funiciello claims that the emphasis on service over direct income redistribution to the poor masks the massive redistribution of wealth to middle-class poverty pimps. The poverty industry expanded so much during the 1980s that social service agencies and programs actually had to compete for clients. But that was not the only reason that clients were scarce. According to Funiciello, service providers and recipients were engaged in a struggle over the right to represent the interests of the poor:

> The toughest adversaries of welfare mothers who organized for their rights were often those in the "not for profit" charity organizations. These functioned in a kind of vulterine relation to poor people. Their very survival depended upon the existence of poor people. In theory, they were "allies." In fact, as agents of the status quo, they couldn't sell poor women out fast enough. (Or buy some, advertise them in their promotional literature, and parade them around like tamed savages, living testimony to the power of social work.) Sometimes they were even well-intentioned. Class and cultural barriers combined with their paychecks made it all but impossible for them

to understand poor women at all, much less represent their interests. Active [activist] welfare mothers who tried to hold on to their own agendas without getting walloped by "helping hands" were universally skeptical of the do-good agencies. They had been all been "helped" at least once too often.[48]

Contra Murray, Funiciello argues that recipients are well aware that welfare does not serve their interests. In fact, her book is filled with anecdotes about women who did not act as the system expected them to. *The Tyranny of Kindness* opens with the story of Fatima Ali, who threw her children out the window rather than face a life of impoverished single-motherhood. From the morbid to the heroic, the devious to the courageous, the range of resistance that Funiciello documents inadvertently demonstrates that the powers of the powerful depend not so much on the exclusion of the poor as on recruiting and retaining the voluntary compliance of their clients in punitive and coercive programs.

But Funiciello does not account for why so many seek and continue to receive "help" that in all actuality, as she herself argues, is no help at all. Although she writes from the perspective of those who suffer the consequences of the poverty industry, the combined causes of ruling-class interests and ideology fail to account for the possibility that a recipient might either refuse or demand "help." Nevertheless, in arguing that power works to serve the interests of the rich by producing the acquiescence and exclusion of the poor, as well as their condition of poverty, she gives evidence in countless examples that refute the social control thesis. When she argues that welfare recipients are excluded, intimidated, and impoverished by the system of welfare and social services, Funiciello fails to recognize the political significance of the fact that welfare programs operate to *promote* autonomy, self-sufficiency, and participation. In her eyes, those objectives are merely an ideological justification for enriching the middle-class poverty pimps, not a rationale for governing the poor.

For example, poverty pimps cannot force a pregnant woman into a prenatal health-care program. Attempts in the 1980s to incarcerate drug addicts during the term of their pregnancy proved unpopular and unsuccessful.[49] Methods to induce women to enter programs voluntarily included gifts of diapers, toys, and cosmetics, all donated by local businesses and offered as inducements to participate in prenatal care. Another was the "Tupperware" model of home parties, where one invites friends to participate in plans to earn free goods.[50] But because such programs operated under intense supervision and control, recruitment was a constant problem.

Funiciello fails to look beyond the (hypothetical) clash of economic interests between recipients and service providers to the political effects of "help." Just the fact that there are poverty pimps does not explain how poor people are governed. Moreover, in her single-minded focus on following the money trail, Funiciello fails to investigate the links between the agencies, the professionals who staff them, and knowledge: in other words, the links between representing the poor, helping the poor, and knowing the poor.

While it is true that those who benefit most from welfare are middle-class service providers, they do so by instrumentalizing the needs of others. I mean to say not that their actions are instrumental in securing their own interests but that they instrumentalize the voice of "the poor." Any claim to know what is best for poor people, to know what it takes to get out of poverty and what needs must be met in order to be fully human, is also a claim to power. Even the silence of the poor can be instrumentalized to represent the poor, as Funiciello herself documents; silence can be heard as a call for new programs to ensure that the voice of "the poor" is heard.

In other words, service providers and caseworkers not only wield power in their own interest; they also act upon the interests of those they "help." In Funiciello's account of the poverty industry, programs are designed in the name of "the poor" without ever so much as consulting poor people about their needs — yet her own evidence suggests that every conceivable effort is made to document poor women's desires and needs in order to turn those desires into an instrument for recruiting. Funiciello aptly uses the vocabulary of market research: "the creation and marketing of homeless people," for example.[51] Recipients do have to be created, however, their social construction is founded not on the abnegation of their real interests but on the production of their interest in helping themsleves.

Making Citizens: Bio-Power

By neglecting the question of how power works and focusing solely on the question of who has the "real" power, Murray and Funiciello miss what I take to be the political significance of welfare: it is a form of government that is both voluntary and coercive. Much more than a way of organizing interests, it is also a way of organizing power, a way of acting on people's actions rather than procuring their apathy. Welfare, bureaucracy, and administration are not modes of governance that cancel out citizenship by producing subjects, dependence, and quiescence. They are modes of government that work upon the capacities of citizens to act on their own behalf.[52]

Democratic governance cannot force its interests but must enlist the willing participation of individuals in the pursuit of its objects. Intervention aims, for example, at transforming the aspirations of drug addicts to those of being good mothers and maintaining custody of their children — for their own good and for the good of all of society. Intervention and prevention work as a kind of recruitment. Even when an economic rationality is brought to bear on a social problem (drug addicts must be made over into self-governing agents in order to spare the state the expense of foster care and treating drug-addicted infants), its method is to govern people by getting them to govern themselves.

To be sure, legislation in several locales would charge those who give birth to addicted babies with criminal neglect. The strategy to prevent harm, however, has so far won out over the strategy of punishment. Despite the fact that many people caught between a drug conviction and a rehab program for pregnant mothers are coerced into participating, the program is still one option of more than one. If they were not voluntary, programs could not claim to represent the interests of those they serve.

A program might attempt to invest a young mother in "parenting." She is encouraged to understand herself as a parent, to prioritize her relationship with her child, and to understand that relationship as a field of action in which she and her child can become empowered. In social programs, coercion can, by definition, never be in anyone's interest.[53] The interests to be served are the autonomy, the well-being, the very life of mother and child.

I am describing here a mode of exercising power, a mode of government, that only rarely resorts to violence. Foucault called the exercise of such power in liberal democratic regimes "bio-power." Bio-power, he wrote, "brought life and its mechanisms into the realm of explicit calculations and made knowledge-power an agent of the transformation of human life."[54] The political rationality of bio-power turns human needs, welfare, and desires into the terrain of governance. Bio-power renders life itself governable, making it possible to act not only upon the body, by force, but also upon the subjectivity (soul) of human being.[55]

"The professionalization of being human," as Funiciello put it, does not pit the interests of the experts against the interests and self-knowledge of the people. Rather, bio-power, through the administration and regulation of life and its needs, enacts the good of all society upon the antisocial bodies of the poor, deviant, and unhealthy. It seeks to unite the interests of the individual with the interests of society as a whole (a strategy I described in the introduction).

The health, education, and welfare of the people constitute a territory upon which it is possible to act. Solutions to the problems of poverty and need can be tried out only after the problem of poverty is transformed into a set of possible actions. For example, to declare a war on poverty, drugs, or garbage is to say that these fields are open to action, places upon which it is possible to act, and where government might intervene. To wage a war on human need is to extend the reach of bio-power, to mobilize knowledge and power on the terrain of poverty, hunger, violence, or drugs.

As I have noted, Foucault defined government broadly as "the conduct of conduct," an "ensemble formed by the institutions, analyses and reflections, the calculations and tactics, that allow the exercise of this very specific albeit complex form of power."[56] All those experts and agencies that are authorized to intervene in the life of a pregnant crack addict, for example — doctors, police, therapists, judges, child protection officials—are involved in making up the ensemble.[57] The ways poor people are governed very often have little to do with state power except when, for example, the national guard is brought in. More often, poor people are governed at the level of the social through case management, empowerment programs, parenting classes, and work training. Again, constituting the needs and interests of others to fulfill their human potential is a mode of governing people.[58]

For social problems to be territorialized, they must be known. For government to solve the "social problems" of poverty, delinquency, dependency, crime, self-esteem, and so on, it must have a certain kind of knowledge that is measurable, specific, and calculable, knowledge that can be organized into governmental solutions. Social scientific knowledge is central to the government of the poor, to the very formation of the poor as an identifiable group (see Chapter 3), and to the formation of the domain of social government. Foucault suggests that the beginning of modern forms of government is marked by "new methods of power whose operation is not ensured by right but by technique, not by law but by normalization, not by punishment but by control, methods that are employed on all levels and in forms that go beyond the state and its apparatus."[59]

Following Foucault, I argue that the subjectivity of the citizen is the object and the outcome of government. That is not to say that no subjectivity exists prior to government, for that would be to say that government produces subjects, not citizens. I am concerned here with a form of power that promotes rather than represses subjectivity, power that produces and relies upon active subjects rather than absolute subjugation. Instead of excluding participation or repressing subjectivity, bio-power operates to invest the citizen with a set of goals and self-understandings, and gives the citizen-subject an investment in participating voluntarily in programs, projects, and institutions set up to "help" them.

Acquiescence and rebellion are not antithetical but can take place in the same breath. I originally began writing in a vein similar to Funiciello's, declaring that poor women on welfare are excluded from meaningful participation and explaining how undemocratic, racist, and punitive welfare is, particularly AFDC. It took me many years of activism to realize that the blatant injustice of welfare is just that — blatant, obvious. There is no contradiction, no set of facts to marshal against the pervasive myths, no underlying and liberating truths to expose. My vantage point has changed: welfare recipients are not excluded or controlled by power so much as constituted and put into action by power.

Murray and Funiciello, although they hope to transform welfare recipients from subjects into citizens, simply repeat the "truth" that they are subjects — socially constructed, controlled, and manipulated. Yet revealing the "true" causes of their subordination cannot help to treat recipients as citizens. I am arguing that welfare does not cause citizens to behave in one way or another. Rather, as Foucault puts it, welfare "structures the possible field of action by others."[60] Which is to say that welfare recipients are already citizens, fully capable of action.

This is a messy argument to make. No one says this better than John Marr, the fictional narrator of Samuel Delany's novel *The Mad Man*, in his account of the life of Timothy Hasler, a fictional philosopher:

> But what is inchoate in Hasler's work, from beginning to end — what he best represents — is the realization that large-scale, messy, informal systems are necessary in order to develop, on top of them, precise, hard-edged, tractable systems; more accurately, structures that are so informal it's questionable whether they can be called systematic at all are prerequisites for those structures that can, indeed, be recognized as systems in the first place. . . . For Hasler, the messy is what provides the energy which holds any system within it coherent and stable.[61]

Hasler, then, subverts the causal order found in Funiciello and Murray's arguments for the abolition of welfare. He also suggests to me that welfare is not the cause of dependence and poverty but the effect of messy, non-generalizable, and contingent practices, institutions, and discourses — not whole systems. Social construction is just not that simple or straightforward. The system and its makers do not create order from above; rather, the messiness of small things makes possible a large system like welfare.

The Liberal Arts of Governance

The social is an enigmatic and worrying figure of which no one wants to take stock for fear of losing one's way or one's Lenin.

JACQUES DONZELOT

But society equalizes under all circumstances, and the victory of equality in the modern world is only the political and legal recognition of the fact that society has conquered the public realm, and that distinction and difference have become private matters of the individual.

HANNAH ARENDT

It is along the same line that the points of authoritarianism, the points of reform, the points of resistance and revolution, come face to face around this new stake, "the social."

GILLES DELEUZE

In the associations between the political liberty of all (citizenship) and the subjection of some (the "unfit," "residuum," "dependent," "underclass"), between the self-acting and those who fail to act, and in their solutions to "social problems," nineteenth-century reform societies devised the practical arts of liberal government. The principles guiding the liberal arts of government, as shown in the example of J. A. Hobson, were laid out against utilitarian and rights-based political doctrines. They were derived from political and social theory as much as from the political problems facing liberal states, as the example of T. H. Green (below) illustrates. The practical arts of liberal government, however, were not invented in their totality or centrally administered by the state. It was the invention of "society as a whole" that gave scope to a multitude of particular and localized social programs, to the development of the social sciences and professional social work. The practical arts of government, I argue, gave material form to the abstract space of the social. By illustrating both the principles and the practical arts of government (philanthropy and self-help in particular) and the strategies and techniques of social reform movements, I hope to illuminate both the origins and the limits of the will to empower.

If the advent of the social is the condition that enabled universal citizenship it is also the condition under which democratic citizenship is constrained. Liberal rationalities had their origin long before the nineteenth century, yet it was then that they took on a democratic form. With the gradual granting of citizenship to the population as a whole over the nineteenth and twentieth centuries, exceptions to the rule of the individual's inviolability were still glaringly obvious (slavery, the exclusion of women, age and property restrictions), if less quietly tolerated. Yet with democratic citizenship the people, not the state, were sovereign. A means of democratic government, one that did not violate the will of the people, had to be invented.

Against the grain of totalizing histories of social control and the liberal presumption of voluntarism, I argue that the abstraction "society as a whole" signals a mode of politics that is always in doubt, a politics that is best expressed in oxymora such as voluntary servitude, regulated freedom, and involuntary accord. My aim is to introduce into democratic theory a conception of the social neither as the domain of autonomy and uncoerced association (civil society) nor as the space of domination (social control).[1] Each of those two interpretations of the social tends to situate the sources of citizenship outside the political, whereas I attempt *to resituate politics on the level at which citizens are constituted as free and politically active subjects.*

In the preceding chapter I argued against the idea that welfare is an institution of social control. Here, I argue against two related arguments that social modes of government, administration, and bureaucracy either "politicize" or "depoliticize" relationships of power. Against the antimodernism of Hannah Arendt, I argue that the advent of the social did not *displace* the political but did *refigure* the political. I conclude by reinterpreting the political significance of what Laclau and Mouffe call the "politicization" of the social by "new social movements" in the 1960s.

Society as a Whole

Adam Ferguson, a figure of the Scottish Enlightenment, held that "man" did not emerge from a state of nature and invent society. Against Rousseau, he argued that the history of civil society was a natural one. Spontaneous relations of authority, growing from the different capacities and strengths of persons, developed into forms of political order and government. To Ferguson, the self-regulation of civil society meant that political power was not consensual but was the ongoing result of forming and re-forming authority in civil society. The history of civil society was its own making and re-making.[2] To progress (a development that for Ferguson was not as inevitable as his contemporaries, David Hume and Adam Smith, seemed to imply), civil society must be re-formed continually.[3]

Self-government and civic virtue were values for Ferguson, to be sure, but they could not safely be the ends of intentional re-formation: "Corrupt and vicious men, assembled in great bodies, cannot have a greater curse bestowed upon them, than the power of governing themselves."[4] Any new development of civil society was likely to be unplanned. Ferguson's vision of social re-formation was not given a positive design until social reform and change were rationalized and governmentalized in the nineteenth century.

What the Scottish Enlightenment thinkers did, according to Michel Foucault, was to establish society as an order distinct from the political.[5] Before this, John Locke, for example, had used "civil society" as a synonym for political society, and governmental authority was modeled on the family. After the autonomy of civil society was established, Foucault points out, society became both the limit and terrain of liberal government. The problem for liberal government was to ensure the self-regulation of society without interfering in its progress. To govern an already existing society, government had to become the art of governing indirectly.

By the nineteenth century the preoccupation of social and political theory with the origins of the social had fallen to the social scientific assumption that society was always already there in total. Auguste Comte and Emile Durkheim, for example, treated the social as a causal force with its own natural laws. Bruno Latour, among others, has made this point before: "Sociology had become a positive science only once it stopped bickering about the origins of society and instead started with the notion of an all-embracing society that could then be used to explain various phenomena of interest."[6] The positive sum of those explanations was the social itself. Latour, among others, argues that the social is an effect rather than a cause; it can exist only insofar as it is continually brought into being.

To bring citizens into society, to transform the apathetic into citizens willing and able to govern themselves democratically, reformers reinvented government at the level of the social. British idealists such as T. H. Green,

Bernard Bosanquet, and Helen Bosanquet, among others, theorized "positive liberalism," a method of indirect government that split the difference between positive and negative liberty.[7] The "negative liberty" so dear to J. S. Mill was to Green a manner of pitting the individual against the state. On the negative liberty of individuals, Green wrote, "It is only when this liberty is interfered with that any occasion arises for an explanation of the compatibility of the sovereign's right with the natural right of the individual; and it is just then that the explanation of the supposition that the right of the sovereign is founded on consent, fails."[8] Indeed, Green rejected natural rights as a "fiction" and believed that negative liberty undermined the very possibility of legitimate government. Instead, he grounded positive rights in the prior existence of civil society.

Positive liberty was not the opposite of negative liberty. Green did not assert the positive rights of individuals against the state but, rather, that the positive right of the individual to act in a manner consistent with the common good served as a regulatory principle. Positive liberty did not entail a paternalist state that could force the citizen to act for the common good.[9] Far from it — for once an action was forced, it was no longer a matter of the citizen's own will, no longer a free action.

The individual and the state could not be at odds if the will of each was directed toward the good of all. How could the state ensure that individual wills would go in the direction of the common good without coercion? Green held that society was both the source and the result of positive rights. He argued that the voluntary actions and desires of individuals formed society. Society could never make a claim on individuals to act against their own desire because that would undermine the sources of civil society. So long as individuals acted in the interest of their own well-being, they would be acting in the interest of society. Each one "must, in short, be capable of conceiving and seeking a permanent well-being in which the permanent well-being of others is included."[10]

But what of the case where individuals do not act in the interest of their own well-being? Habitual drunkenness, for example, said Green, could not be in anyone's interest. If the state interfered with the desire to get drunk by outlawing alcohol, the individual's desire would not change by being restrained. In that case, the individual's right was pitted against the state: any obedience to the state's law would be given not freely, but only out of fear of sanction. The capacity for rights "is a capacity which cannot be generated — which on the contrary is neutralized — by any influence that interferes with the spontaneous action of social interests."[11] Such a law would undermine the capacities of individuals to exercise their rights still further.

States could and should make laws that might have the appearance of constraint in such cases, but those laws must be administered in such a way as to enhance the capacities of individuals to act voluntarily for the common good. The state could not legislate morality, but it could legislate in order to prevent harm. Green developed several well-worn test scenarios. For example, although it may be immoral for parents to fail to educate their child, there is nothing that the state should do about that. The state can, however, prevent the child from growing up without the capacity to act freely, which would in part be due to a lack of education. To prevent harm to the child, then, the state may enforce the education of children.

Despite appearances to the contrary, Green was not begging the question. The parent could choose to have the child educated by the church or by private tutor. The parent was not told *what* to do or not to do, or which education the child must have. Rather, the parent was compelled to do *something*. The law "is from the beginning only felt as compulsion by those in whom, so far as this social function is concerned, there is no spontaneity to be interfered with."[12] In this case, the parent's will would not be directly acted upon; neither would the child feel compelled to go to school against his or her will. But the parent who did not will anything at all was a serious political problem. The failure to will, then, and the failure to act marked the terrain of state intervention.

Green asserted that there is freedom in self-restraint but not in restraint by others. Any obedience to the state or to the common good must be "free obedience," voluntarily and actively given; cooperation must be active rather than passive compliance.[13] Green claimed the right of the state to promote morality, but not the right of the state to determine the moral course. The state must act only to strengthen the moral capacities of individuals, to make it possible for them to restrain themselves, never to determine their ends.

How could the state calculate such a subtle distinction? If all obedience was to be self-imposed, if all moral restraint was to be self-restraint, from what did this capable self derive? From society, of course, but not from the state. The indirect administration of morality and society was not spelled out in detail by Green, but its principles were. It took a regiment of women, as we will see, to transform those principles into techniques of government.

Governing the Poor: Reform Movements and Self-Help

⌈I take self-help to be emblematic of the liberal arts of government; it is a technique for reforming both society and the individual by indirectly harmonizing their interests.⌉

For better or for worse, here and in Chapter 4 I outline self-help as a mode of government that works through the maximization of citizenship.⌉In the hands of nineteenth-century reformers, self-help presented a solution to the "social problems" of poverty, dependence, charity, and immorality. Self-help serves here as an example of how the individual citizen is instrumentally linked to "society as a whole." Moreover, it is a philanthropic technique that is exemplary of modern government⌉it is both voluntary and coercive.⌉

Rather than giving a full account of Victorian philanthropy, I focus only upon self-help and only in the middle- to late Victorian period. The first object of reform for Octavia Hill and others of the Charity Organization Society (COS) was to bring an end to Christian charity. Such charity encouraged the dependence of the poor upon the rich, Hill argued, as well as confirming the status of the rich over and above the poor. The COS aimed to coordinate and rationalize charity so that it was less random and would no longer reproduce or ritualize class divisions.

Hill ardently believed that help was not what those in need needed, so to speak; what they needed was to help themselves, "to be brought back to independence." In her characteristically forbidding style, she explained to an audience of "volunteer visitors among the poor" her reasoning on charity and alms: "First of all, I think they really make them poorer. Then I think they degrade them and make them less independent. Thirdly, I think they destroy the possibility of really good relations between you and them. . . . You want to know [the poor], to enter their lives, their thoughts; . . . you might collect their savings; you might sing for and with them . . . and make them cleaner.[14] Hill had first to change the desire of the visitors to help others as a matter of Christian duty which, she argued, was inspired by the self-interested desire on the part of the rich to do good, to perform one's duty before God. The act of Christian charity ritualized the class order; it inspired awe and deference in the helped and arrogance in the helper. Hill sought a means to incorporate the poor into society so that the power and charity of the wealthy could no longer secure the acquiescence of the poor. The motivations of middle-class Christian charity and duty to the poor had the unintended and irrational effect of producing a permanent class of dependent poor. Instead of helping the poor, middle-class women in particular should seek out ways to get the poor to help themselves. By displacing the helper, self-help was a technique for helping others that could be undertaken in the interests of the poor themselves.

Self-help displaced the ritual of power in interclass relationships and obstructed the ruling-class desire to express power over others. In the same act, Hill found a means to express the will to empower, to overcome working-class resistance and hostility to middle-class home visitors, and to transform the visitor from an intrusive do-gooder into a friend. Her goal was to eradicate class prejudice on both sides. Self-help unified the will to empower and the interests of the poor in a seamless relationship. By conducting the conduct of the poor rather than repressing them, Hill found a means for the will to empower to create social solidarity between the classes.

The methods of self-help were punitive and coercive, but they were now undertaken in the interest of the helped. "In nearly every case requiring help there is some such step of *self*-help which ought to be taken by the family itself, or a member of it."[15] Hill listed some possibilities, including putting a daughter out to service or a son out to "a place," or moving the family to cheaper lodging. The isolation of individual members of a family, in other words, was a method of self-help. The sacrifices that were demanded of poor people would be understood, Hill assured her audience, as a sign of respect from visitors who believed in the capacity and will of the poor to help themselves.

Again, they could not be *made* to help themselves, for then the results would last only as long as the application of force. A genuine solution to the social problems of poverty and class inequality must be sought in self-help. "For I do not myself believe that we from above can help the people so thoroughly and well in any other way as by helping them to help themselves. This I think they are meant to do — this I believe they can do by association and by forethought."[16] (I discuss the "science of association" in Chapter 4.) To get the poor to reason, to think of their long-term interests, and to moralize their actions, one must recruit rather than force them into the activity of helping themselves. The art of liberal government needed to be democratic.

Mary Poovey has written about the same logic as it was applied to selling, rather than giving away, Bibles as a means of engaging the poor in their own evangelization. Techniques of self-help underwent constant revision and contestation among reformers. Ellen Ranyard's Female Bible Mission (1857) altered the methods of distributing Bibles and clothing in order to get the poor to invest in their own well-being. She insisted that Bibles be purchased rather than given as gifts; they must be sold by the poor to the poor so that they might more effectively reach one another. Ranyard's technique of self-help, Poovey suggests, was distinguished from similar efforts by "her recognition that the poor could best be encouraged to help themselves if they were initially helped by another like themselves."[17] Hill, on the other hand, believed that visitors should learn from the poor how to help (much as Colonel Waring learned from the ragpickers). Visitors had to live among and go among the poor, where they would learn to abstain from helping: "Those who love the poor and know them individually will [abstain] more and more in the time to come." Rather than giving money or gifts, one must "give *oneself*" to the poor.[18] Clearly, relations of power were not ultimately settled by self-help. Reformers continued to seek out new techniques for altering the relationship between helpers and the helped.

Hill was determined to avoid giving help or charity in the wrong way; to avoid doing harm, the home visitor must thoroughly know the poor. Their different circumstances and their characters must be classified and counted. "My people are numbered; not merely counted, but known, man, woman, and child."[19] The relationship between those who help and those who are helped to help themselves had to be intimate, and the knowledge derived from that intimacy had to be carefully and faithfully "investigated" and recorded in case records.

Hill had faith that the antisocial poor could be incorporated into society. A given case of poverty, however, could be caused either by poor character and habit or by poor circumstances and temporary bad luck, and to treat both cases the same was to do more harm than good. It was not enough to help others, to fulfill their needs or secure their living conditions. Their capabilities had to be thoroughly investigated in order to make a decision about what should be done. Through social investigation, home visiting, and surveillance, reformers attempted to reach that delicate balance between governing too little and too much, to govern by maximizing the will of the governed rather than determining it.

To unite knowledge of the poor with action, Hill suggested that a secretary be assigned to coordinate and systematize volunteers' efforts to help. The secretary would not visit the poor; her task would be to keep case records and make them available to volunteers. She would also consult with various authorities — police, church officials, school board officers — on particular cases. She would not only supply a record of past decisions regarding a case "but afterwards, when the decision was made and relief granted or withheld, through succeeding years she would get the people watched over with that continuous care without which right decisions at any particular crisis of life lose half their efficacy; indeed, she might often avert such a crisis altogether."[20] The surveillance of the poor, then, was to be ongoing, even without their application for assistance; prevention soon replaced intervention as the watchword of reform. In other words, knowledge was continually gathered but indirectly applied. No appeal for help was necessary, since the interests and needs of the poor were represented in their case records.

This activity was not directed in the interest of forming a permanent profession for middle-class women or of giving free reign to the will to empower. Although those *were* two effects of the development of social work, Hill herself made a case against forming a profession or bureaucracy for helping the poor: "If we establish a system of professed workers, we shall quickly begin to hug our system, and perhaps to want to perpetuate it even to the extent of making work for it."[21] There were no general rules for helping; the details of each case carried the information necessary for determining the best course of help, and each case must be treated individually and systematically.[22] The system of relief could not be generalized or governed by principles, only by direct intervention and personal knowledge of case histories.

Still, the detailed knowledge of individuals and families held in case records did eventually displace the home visitor altogether, once statistical projections of the needs and failings of the poor were generated without physical contact. Moreover, self-help was designed to lift the people out of themselves, to get them to objectify their own selves so that they would have no further need to be the objects of help. The displacement of the home visitor was a logical development in the rationalization of self-help. Yet however indirect the relationship of power between the helper and the helped, it was still a relationship of power that took two to enter, and resistance and reticence on the part of the poor did not disappear.

The resistance of poor people to home visitors and Poor Law officials and any class resentment of "do-gooders" had to be overcome somehow. Even harder to surmount than their discontent and rebellion was the indifference of the poor. Helen Bosanquet, whose tenure in COS followed Hill's and who oversaw the professionalization of social work that Hill had resisted, sought a new solution: "It is to the discontented that the would-be innovator of every description addresses himself — the socialist, the anarchist, the vegetarian, the atheist, and all the multitude who have a favorite social remedy to push. But discontent is only another form of living in the present. . . . The one interest which has power to carry them out of themselves is politics."[23]

To lift the people out of the present, to get them to use foresight and aim high, required that their discontent and their indolence be turned to "useful citizenship."[24] What was the method by which the discontent of the people could be made useful without force or manipulation and without determining its direction? That is, how could the people be governed without state action? How was it possible to instrumentalize the interests and actions of individuals without turning them into mere instruments?

For Bosanquet, what was needed was a means of harnessing individual wills to the wheel of social progress that did not entail the political repression of the working classes. It was their action that she was concerned to corral, not their quiescence. "I like to picture humanity as a great army pressing onwards towards an invisible goal, and guided by a wisdom not its own."[25] Whose wisdom? The anonymous wisdom of social conventions that led society spontaneously toward progress. But where was all this "social progress" headed? By what principle was it to be guided?

Bosanquet's solution, the "Standard of Life," would seem to offer a fixed and rigidly middle-class standard by which the poor should be measured and governed, but it was in fact a standard set against the aristocratic tendency to judge and to rule the poor by their own class standards. Because the occupations of the poor were different from their own, the higher classes perceived the very nature of the poor as different. The prejudice that there was more than one class and therefore more than one society led traditionalists to assert a permanent antagonism between the classes. Bosanquet objected; despite the fact that different people followed different standards, there was still only one Standard of Life in the sense that all strove to fulfill some standard. "We may of course allow that the working classes have disadvantages to contend against . . . but we must in common justice recognize this power of determining their own standard of life and of working toward it in their own way."[26] It was necessary to overcome resistance on the part of all classes in order to practice the art of self-help.

The Standard of Life was not a fixed moral standard; in fact, it was "incapable of exact definition; in other words, its significance is inexhaustible, for it has not yet become stereotyped into one narrow usage."[27] The problem for Bosanquet was not that the poor lacked conformity to one true standard but that they were judged too often by bourgeois standards.

Bosanquet told a story about how the standard of life works by comparing it to a unit of measurement. On a stone wall in Trafalgar Square, she said, is "something so important that it is hardly ever looked at," and few even know it is there.[28] It is the standard of measurements — furlong, yard, foot, and inch — carved in the stone, determining what would be called "a foot," "a yard," and so on. It is a standard that is used every day without thought, anonymously guiding relations of exchange. It just is. Few wonder where it came from, and fewer still would think to challenge it or revise it. But it is there, and normal daily activities and progress would be impossible without it. Indeed, agreement on the standard is implicit in its use; otherwise measurement would be an infinite source of conflict. When we measure, we concern ourselves not with the accuracy of "a foot" but with whatever it is we are measuring against the standard. Such is the case with the Standard of Life. We do not pursue our standard blindly so much as we have no need to examine it. The Standard of Life works to make the actions of individuals, despite their lack of conformity, move in the same way.

This is consistent with how Foucault characterized normalization and bio-power, which depend upon the operationalization of an illusive norm that is nowhere actually defined. Because it is an illusive good, the Standard of Life unites the diverse interests of individuals with the uniform interest of society as a whole. It is at once, in Foucault's framing, individualizing and totalizing. Class interests and pursuits need not conflict if each is directed toward the progress of society as a whole. If each self, regardless of class, pursued his or her own Standard of Life, then the class-divided society could be transformed into a classless society, and, needless to say, that would be progress.

Self-interest could work as an instrument of social progress only if it was understood as the pursuit, rather than the restraint, of desire and difference. Echoing the words of T. H. Green, Bosanquet wrote: "We cannot force interests of occupations or benefits of any kind upon men from without, however desirable we may think them; they must grow out of their own strivings and desires, their own planning and progress. The best we can do for each other is to remove unnecessary obstacles, and the worst — to weaken any of the motives which urge us to strive."[29] Only the most "indirect" forms of governance could avoid making things worse.[30] To change the social order and to quiet class conflicts, then, it was necessary that government operate in such a way as to maximize the strivings of each and all.

There was one important social distinction to be made, however. Between the people that strive and those that do not, Bosanquet saw a vast divide. Even in a classless society, those in the "Residuum," a kind of small underclass, could not be helped because they simply had no desires beyond mere survival or the next drink. They had no selves, so to speak, to help, no Standard of Life to reach for; they were indifferent to their own lives.

"The Residuum" was certainly a moral designation, but any attempt to redeem that class would be dangerous: "After all is said and done, organization is only one among many means of self-help; it is impossible to organize dead matter from the outside, and the true Residuum is economically dead. It may be possible to galvanize it into a temporary appearance of life, to raise up a social monster that will be the terror of the community; but the best that can really be hoped for is that it should gradually wear itself away."[31] The existence of the Residuum was a threat to progress. Yet, Bosanquet was quite sure it posed no lasting threat so long as it was not acted upon. Because those in the Residuum had no desires, it would fail to progress and would wither away. What positioned them outside society as a whole was not that they had the wrong values but that they had no values. The rest of the poor could be incorporated into society so long as they strove for something, whatever it might be.

Rather than merely producing desired behavior and conformity or "depoliticizing" class inequality, the technique of self-help relies upon action and difference. Without the different standards held by individuals, the progress of society would grind to a halt. And still, those differences of interest and desire need not produce conflict so long as they are all directed by a Standard of Life. Self-help is not a technique of government that can be adequately described in terms of either positive or negative liberty, action or behavior, citizenship or subjection. It aims to make the poor into citizens through their voluntary subjection to their own interests and to the Standard of Life.

Society as a Whole and Political Freedom

Rather than a technique of social control, I am arguing, self-help is a means of instrumentalizing and maximizing the self-interest of the poor. While it excludes those held to have no self-interest, it works to incorporate the rest. Individual freedom was both a premise and a limit of self-help schemes. The danger was to encroach upon individual freedom by acting too much or too little. Hence, self-help schemes underwent constant revision and reform.

The necessity of reform reveals that political order changes not only during exceptional times of political upheaval but as a matter of course.[32] The political importance of reform societies follows from their continual re-forming of the relationships between public and private, personal and political, political and social. Self-help is not strictly a social or a personal relationship but one that changes the nature of society and the person. Self-help is a political relationship, a technique for solving political problems such as poverty and class conflict. Rather than negating the autonomy and action of citizens, social government is a means of promoting and instrumentalizing citizenship and autonomy.

The liberal arts of government are applied not only to the administration of the state but to the management of the economy, the population, children, the poor, and the sick. Liberal "rationalities of government," as Foucault said, are methods for "the conduct of the conduct" of others and oneself.[33] Under liberalism, the inviolability of the economy and the individual mean that the state can not directly govern their domains, the economic and the private. The most typical manifestation of liberal rationalities, of course, is an argument for limiting the size and number of the state's interventions into society, e.g., self-government.

Self-help provides a solution to political problems that do not require state action, conformity to society, or the repression of dissent. In fact, by enlarging the scope and reign of individuals, self-help is a technique that works to limit the need for state action — not by "depoliticizing" class relations or excluding the poor from politics but by getting them to act.

Quite another view of the social, in the enormously influential work of Hannah Arendt, is as a homogeneous and homogenizing "blob."[34] Arendt's condemnation of the social as a scourge upon the political is an important source of the failure of democratic theory to see the social as a source of the transformation of the political in modernity. In her view, the political cannot be resituated vis-à-vis the social and the private without losing its character altogether. She treated each as a distinctive sphere locked in a zero-sum game with the others. Arendt, whose writings have provoked several critical oppositions leveled by democratic theorists, argues that the "rise of the social" meant the decline of public life. When the elements of the social, especially the economy and the family, became public, private interests and personal differences crowded out a purely political concern for the political order. Indeed, she suggests, the fact that the family ceased to serve as a model for political rule "may also be due to a development in which society devoured the family unit until it became a full-fledged substitute for it."[35] "Social housekeeping" supplanted political rule as well as the private rule of the family. The political disappeared and along with it the possibility of freedom.

Arendt argues that the social was the space of a tyrannical mode of government, the social was a realm of "Rule by Nobody." But this nobody "does not cease for having lost its personality. As we know from the most social form of government, that is, from bureaucracy, . . . the rule by nobody is not necessarily no-rule; it may indeed, under certain circumstances, even turn out to be one of its cruelest and most tyrannical versions."[36] To be sure, Arendt had cause for alarm. In her mind, totalitarianism was the result of the thoughtlessness of bureaucratic rule. She believed that "rule by nobody" signaled the complete domination of *homo politicus*, a kind of tyranny exercised not by a tyrant but by the encroachment of the social into the one possible space of freedom and action: the political.

Arendt draws the line between the social and the political to mark off the realms of behavior and action, respectively. Behavior, the outcome of discipline and "normalization," is opposed to the freedom possible only in the public realm: "It is decisive that society, on all its levels, excludes the possibility of action. . . . Instead, society expects from each of its members a kind of behavior, imposing innumerable and various rules, all of which tend to 'normalize' its members, to make them behave, to exclude spontaneous or outstanding achievement."[37] Whereas the public is the realm of action and individual plurality, the social is a realm of behavior and individual conformity. The separate character of these realms, for Arendt, permanently fixed the potentials for human-being in each one. The political could not be re-formed or even refigured without losing the space of freedom.

Arendt goes so far as to present conflict in the terms of whole "realms" at war: "The social realm, where the life process has established its own public domain, has let loose an unnatural growth, so to speak, of the natural; and it is against this growth, not merely against society but against the constantly growing social realm, that the private and the intimate, on the one hand, and the political (in the narrower sense of the word), on the other, have proved incapable of defending themselves."[38]

Such passages read as if the social realm were a pernicious weed rather than a "hybrid."[39] But these organic metaphors foreclose discussion of the possibility that politics itself sets the borders of the political. As I have been arguing, the social and the political, like subjectivity, cannot be properly understood outside the conditions of their own production. Arendt cannot see that the social is a product of human action, not simply a realm of behavior, because she sets in absolute opposition the political capacity to act and the behavior produced in the social realm.

For Arendt, politics is an external field occupied by the citizen engaged in creating reality, what she calls "worldliness." For the creature of the social and the private, reality is a dead weight, unalterable and therefore such a creature has no place and no politics but merely inhabits "worldlessness." The political excludes those aspects of life that are private, natural, bodily, habitual, social, economic, or familial. The social, Arendt argues, is neither public nor private. The advent of the social "brought about the simultaneous decline of the public as well as the private realm."[40] Arendt despised this development and mourned the loss of the one authentically political creation of "man": a truly political public sphere of action and freedom.

Like Tocqueville before her, Arendt sees the possibility of a completely new and terrible tyranny in democratic equality, in a "rule by nobody" that blurs the lines between the public and the private: "Society equalizes under all circumstances, and the victory of equality in the modern world is only the political and legal recognition of the fact that society has conquered the public realm, and that distinction and difference have become the private matters of the individual."[41] Rather than a measure of progress, equality is a measure of how far a society has devolved from the ideal of the Greek polis. Arendt imagines that without a truly political public sphere of action, human plurality will disappear or devolve further into mere difference — what we call "diversity" today.

The loss of "the political" operates for Arendt as a critical mark of modernity. Democratic theory will not be reconciled to mass democracy, however, so long as the Greek standards of the political are used to judge contemporary politics. Arendt equates the rise of the social with the loss of political reality altogether rather than with a new mode of constituting political reality. In other words, she assumes that there is a unity conferred by one or another of these regimes, the political or the social-bureaucratic.

It is a misnomer to classify Arendt as a democrat, in part because for her the existence of the political has no necessary relation to democratic government.[42] Rather, the political precedes any particular form of government. The political itself cannot survive the institutionalization of the space of appearance. In the political, there is no place for government, only for action.[43]

The critical distinction between the political and the social leaves no room for the possibility that the political might be reinvented, relocated or re-formed. Indeed, in her view, the political can not be reinvented, because it is itself the condition of possibility for political invention. In other words, the political is not just the sphere of politics but the origin of genuine politics. Once again, to see either the social or political as anything other than an effect of human action is to foreclose the possibility of new re-formations.

Arendt refuses to entertain the possibility that political action might be taken to relocate the political in new relationships to the social and the private. In fact, however, the unity of the social assumed by Arendt is the outcome of innumerable changes in the techniques and strategies of government. Her critical opposition of the political and the social is misleading; to understand the possibilities for democracy, we need to call the assumption of separate spheres — public and private, state and civil society — into question.

There are other means by which democratic antiliberalism might critically confront the subjective aspects of citizenship under liberal government. The liberal arts of government do act upon the subjective capacities of citizens, not in any sinister way but through governmental techniques grounded in the social. The individual's will and freedom to act are brought into line with the social good not through their negation but through the activation and maximization of the individual's will. These techniques are changeable and within reach politically without recourse to "the political." The rise of the social does not *necessarily* signal the end of difference and distinction or total conformity; it may even signify a new means of constituting human plurality.[44] Indeed, one of the reasons Arendt deplores the rise of "social housekeeping" is that women (unequals) have found their way into public life through the arts of liberal government.

Governing and Guiding Women

The social was and is the province of women and feminist reformers in particular. "The new breed of governing and guiding women," in Beatrice Webb's phrase, organized and entered social life through philanthropy.[45] Indeed, the phrase "municipal housekeeping" was applied to sanitary reform in part because of the large number of female reformers who took responsibility for cleaning up the garbage and pollution in their cities. One report from 1897 explains why women involved themselves in indirect forms of government: "Every attempt on the part of women to benefit the public is necessarily somewhat indirect. They do not hold the ballot, nor sit in legislative halls. . . . Their part in public reforms is chiefly suggestive or cooperative."[46] The exclusion of women from politics does not entirely explain their social activism, however.

Denise Riley, to whose account of the social my own work is deeply indebted, suggests that middle-class women emerged as collective subjects of politics alongside the invention of the social as a field of intervention into the lives of poor women.[47] It was not only because women (meaning then middle-class women) were excluded from the political that they acted within the social. It was also the case that middle-class women and other excluded populations "lacked a stake in maintaining the status quo."[48] Among the excluded, however, the stakes of middle-class women were uniquely invested in the will to empower.[49]

Feminist and social historians have documented middle-class women's entry into public-political life as social reformers, philanthropists, and charity workers.[50] Of course, prostitutes and working-class women had appeared in public long before there was woman suffrage. As Riley argues, the social enabled women's activism even as it limited the political solidarity of "women" to the claim that women are naturally more benevolent helpers than men. What seems of great significance here is that feminism was caught up at the outset in the development of the liberal arts of government.

Feminists today need not construct an alternative vision of the welfare state so much as to confront the feminist and feminine legacy of social government. The feminist problem with government is still caught within the basic dilemma of liberal government. It is most familiar in its philanthropic guise: how can feminists help poor and disenfranchised women when those women cannot or will not articulate their own needs in the form of political demands? And when they do, how is it possible to meet those needs without constituting poor women as needful? What should be done when women refuse to act politically to represent themselves? The feminist problem with governance can be posed in many different ways, most notably in terms of "the man in the state" or the public sphere, as Wendy Brown and Nancy Fraser do, respectively.[51] It can also be posed in terms of the will to empower embedded in practical relations of help.

It is much too common in democratic and feminist theory to shirk the question of governing by insisting upon the centrality of politics. For example, Nancy Fraser describes the professionalization of the movement to aid battered women, but she does not critically assess the techniques that feminists have invented to compel battered women to act in their own self-interest.[52] She skirts the question of feminist government when she opposes "the tendency for the politics of need interpretation to devolve into the administration of need satisfaction."[53] The trade-off, as Fraser sees it, is between two interpretations of need; battered women's expression of their own needs and political demands, and the professional interpretation of those needs. By dichotomizing "politics" and "administration," Fraser conceives of administration as the antithesis of a genuine feminist politics. Permanently deferring the problem of government, she calls for an alternative vision of a future and more nearly perfect (radically democratic, socialist, or feminist) welfare state; she does not call for new techniques of government, just new principles of government.

If feminists are to counter the successes of neoliberal reforms effectively, we cannot choose between defending and attacking the welfare state. Recall from the introduction my account of the activist's version of the welfare trap. Feminists must critically assess our own methods, in Beatrice Webb's phrase, of "governing and guiding" other women. Another way to say this is that feminism's will to empower other women must undergo some intense scrutiny. The problem for feminists is not *whether* to help other women but *how*; what form should helping take? The question is not whether feminists should defend the welfare state or come up with an alternative vision of it, but how feminists can reinvent the mode of government we call "help" and "welfare."[54]

Wendy Brown points out that the feminist left once attacked the disciplinary and constitutive relationship of women to the state. She calls the recent turn in feminism to defending the welfare state, particularly by Frances Fox Piven and Barbara Ehrenreich, a "retreat from the politics of domination within capitalism."[55] Brown poses the question to Piven, "Do these expanding relationships [of women to the state] produce only active *political* subjects, or do they produce regulated, subordinated, and disciplined *state* subjects?"[56]

Piven indirectly answers Brown's question: "I think it is an undiscriminating antipathy to the state that is wrong, for it is based on a series of misleading and simplistic alternatives. On the one hand, there is the possibility of power and autonomy; on the other, dependence and a controlling state. But these polarities are unreal: All social relationships involve elements of social control, and yet there is no possibility for power except in social relationships."[57] It would seem that in this answer, Piven is the more Foucaultian. That matters only in the sense that although Piven agrees with Brown that women's subjectivities are constrained by the conditions of their production in the welfare state, Piven holds — as do I — that the constitutive powers of the state do not *determine* women's subjectivity.

The feminist turn from an anti-statist to a defensive posture vis-à-vis the state is not new. When the left first rejected Nixon's plan for a national guaranteed income, the Family Assistance Plan (FAP), it did so in the name of an inarticulate rebellion on the part of the masses. The National Welfare Rights Organization (NWRO) joined unions in lobbying hard against FAP because it included work requirements, the minimum income was set too low, and the plan jeopardized administrative due process. NWRO leader George Wiley, with the grassroots membership fading, led the fight against FAP, a position many welfare activists later came to regret. Currently, the call for a guaranteed income nearly defines the left position on welfare reform.

As another example, consider the transformation of the women's movement in the Victorian era to repeal the Contagious Diseases Act. The repeal movement defended the political liberty of prostitutes against the British government's plan to adopt the "French" system whereby doctors and police were empowered to examine prostitutes medically and to keep public records on them. Judith Walkowitz's history of the repeal movement illustrates that the act transformed prostitution from a seasonal and temporary occupation into a profession that divided prostitutes from the working class and from alternative occupations.[58] Soon after feminists won the repeal, the movement was itself transformed into the Social Purity Movement, which called for the protection of women and the prevention of prostitution by the state.

Finally, consider the recent transformation of feminist sexual politics. From the demand for women's control over their own bodies and women's sexual autonomy, second-wave feminism divided into sectarian camps: "pro-sex" on one hand, on the other the "anti-pornography" demand for state censorship and the state regulation of sexuality.[59]

These examples illustrate that there is more at stake for feminists in the politics of welfare reform than the left's betrayal of itself or of working-class women. The enigma for feminism is not the state but the arts of government practiced therein. As Gilles Deleuze noted (see the epigraph above), the left's anti-statism is of one piece with the strong statism it switched to. Liberal democratic society is not wholly the realm of domination and discipline, nor does it contain the promise captured in the slogan "civil society against the state." The critical oppositions between the state and civil society, politics, and administration are misleading. The social is a field of government, a field of possible actions rather than determined outcomes.

The Crisis of Governability

The indeterminism of the social is obvious in the variety of interpretations given to the rise of "new social movements" in the 1960s and the "crisis of governability." The "crisis" was declared by the Trilateral Commission in 1975. By that time, the "democratic surge," as Samuel Huntington labeled the increase in political protest and social movements of the 1960s, had grown into nothing less than a "crisis of democracy." According to Huntington, American democracy is prone to cyclical surges rooted "in the basic American value system and the degree of commitment which groups in society feel toward that value system."[60] In effect, democratic surges realign the relationship between civil society and the state. Huntington suggests that cyclical surges, including those in the Jacksonian and progressive eras, caused a "deepening" of democracy and the expansion of suffrage.

But the 1960s surge was different. It threatened to abolish the distinctions between the state and civil society altogether by calling for democracy in the family, the church, universities, even the military. In other words, following the "democratization" or "politicization" of civil institutions, the sources of citizenship would dry up because they flow only from stable and uncontested institutional authority. With no clear borders protecting civil institutions from political contests, they could no longer supply democratic government with a predictable, reliable, and stable citizenry.

Ironically, Huntington argued, too much democracy spread to civil institutions was bad for democracy. "The vitality of democracy in the United States in the 1960s produced a substantial increase in governmental activity and a substantial decrease in governmental authority."[61] Strong democracy, then, leads to weak democratic government. Put another way, democracy works best when it does not have to "work." "There are," Huntington advised, "potentially desirable limits to the indefinite extension of political democracy. Democracy will have a longer life if it has a more balanced existence."[62]

To restore the necessary balance, Huntington advanced two arguments for limiting democracy. First, the problem of *who* demanded to participate had to be addressed: "The effective operation of a democratic political system usually requires some measure of apathy and noninvolvement on the part of some individuals and some groups."[63] "Some" individuals and "some" groups turned out, of course, to be very specific individuals and groups. Huntington argued that "in the past" the politically active (white elites) were those who had a high regard for the authority of government, and those with "low trust" in government (students, blacks, women) were generally apathetic. The tables hadn't turned, but "democratic distemper" was the result of mixing the two groups in an increasingly polarized political confrontation.[64]

> Marginal social groups, as in the case of blacks, are now becoming full participants in the political system. Yet the danger of overloading the political system with demands which extend its function and undermine its authority still remains. Less marginality on the part of some groups thus needs to be replaced by more self-restraint on the part of all groups.[65]

Thus, a special responsibility fell on the shoulders of blacks to restrain themselves in order to protect democratic stability. Huntington disregarded the fact that the political system was, from the perspective of blacks, not a democratic one in the first place. What was important to him was that the civil rights movement threatened to destabilize the entire political order.

Second, and related, the extension of political participation to students, women, and blacks was a dangerous thing not because those groups overran the political realm but because they threatened to take politics out of the public realm and into previously "nonpolitical" institutions. The problem was no longer to explain the low levels of democratic participation in politics but to explain the increasing demands, particularly on the part of women, ethnic groups, and students, for the democratization of all social institutions: "the family, the university, business, public and private associations, politics, the governmental bureaucracy, and the military services."[66] "Democratic distemper," then, threatened to spread throughout society. Huntington's response was unequivocal: "The arenas where democratic procedures are appropriate are, in short, limited."[67]

The authority crisis of democracy originated not in the realm of government, according to Huntington, but in those institutions that governed effectively *because* they governed undemocratically — including the family, the university, and so on. (Huntington did not mention apartheid or Jim Crow.) These now threatened institutions had once provided the uncontested traditional authority that neutralized whatever instabilities erupted from the democratic participation of white elites. "More precisely, in American society, authority had been commonly based on: organizational position, economic wealth, specialized expertise, legal competence, or electoral representativeness."[68] The social sources of authority threatened to "override the claims of democracy as a way of constituting authority."[69]

The stability of democracy, then, depended upon the nondemocratic organization of power and authority to govern outside the realm of government. Zbigniew Brzezinski, former director of the Trilateral Commission, proposed to "increasingly separate the political system from society and to begin to conceive of the two as separate entities."[70] Society could thus return to a sphere of autonomously formed authority, allowing the state to restore its authority over a restricted public sphere. It was precisely in the arena of the social that the "crisis of governability" was declared.

Whereas Huntington read the signs of crisis to indicate that the United States suffered from too much democracy and participation, Sheldon Wolin read the same signs to indicate a distemper caused by too little (see Chapter 1). Where Huntington saw the dangerous politicization of social institutions and social authority, Wolin saw the "depoliticization" of public-political life. As politics spread throughout social life, the state was abandoned as a source of anything but entitlements. Wolin read these changes as signaling not more democracy but less.

Huntington understood the political implications of the fact that the disciplinary and constitutive functions of social institutions were undergoing an intense transformation. But in Wolin's eyes, the political realm was undergoing an intense depoliticization (or socialization), and the reliance on discipline to govern — as opposed to democratic participation — was growing. But although the two authors disagreed on the details of the crisis, they did agree on its cause: an overflow of politics out of the realm of the state and into the realm of the social.[71]

The debate over the crisis of democracy was, then, over the proper relationship between the state and the social or civil society. Whereas the only form of critique open to Huntington or Wolin was to insist on the specificity of the political and the social, I later explore the possibility that the political and the social have taken on new forms. I understand that historical moment of "crisis" as a missed opportunity for the left to reinvent the liberal arts of government and to reconfigure citizenship by reconfiguring knowledge.[72]

Arendt understood the disciplinary mechanisms of society, such as the Standard of Life and self-help, as means to enforce conformity. The size of mass democracy, along with equality, signaled to her a social form of rule demanding "conformism, behaviorism, and automatism." Indeed, the rise of the social also gave rise to the behavioral, social and statistical sciences which Arendt took as evidence that the social had overgrown the political. "If economics is the science of society in [the social's] early stages . . . the rise of the 'behavioral sciences' indicates clearly the final stage of its development, when mass society has devoured all strata of the nation and 'social behavior' has become the standard for all regions of life."[73] But Arendt assumed that the success of the social sciences and statistics in particular followed *from* the uniformity and conformity that already existed in the realm of the social, as if the categories of behavior were facts independent of the ability of social scientists and statisticians to count them.

Ian Hacking, inspired by Foucault, suggests quite other relationships between politics and numbers, difference and conformity, than those suggested by Arendt. He dates the "avalanche of printed numbers" to around 1820 and argues that the behaviors counted never existed before the practice of counting them brought them into being. "New slots were created in which to fit and enumerate people. Even the national and provincial censuses amazingly show that the categories into which people fall change every ten years. Social change creates new categories of people, but the counting is no mere report of developments. It elaborately, often philanthropically, creates new ways for people to be."[74]

Hacking numbers the statistical sciences as among the productive sciences that link new knowledge to new ways of being. These links signal not the end of action but new possibilities for action on new fields of social life constituted by numbers. The links between behavior and numbers are not links that merely dominate the preexisting capacity of the citizen to act but links that constitute the ability to act.

In Chapter 5 I examine how "governing by numbers" produced the racist and sexist figure of the black welfare queen. Here, I merely seek to underline my argument that the subjectivities of democratic citizens are shaped by social science and governing practices such as self-help. Calculation and categories do not displace or "depoliticize" power so much as put power into operation. I read into the history of social reform and the formation of a "wholly new kind of being" not any "depoliticization" of that being but its very constitution as a political being. The effects of the social organization of power are not repression, exclusion, depoliticization, and domination; the effects of power are embodied in certain kinds of citizens, ways of acting and knowing.

Also, the argument that democratic citizenship depends upon the ability of citizens to keep government at bay are untenable. As I have shown, democratic theorists who pit society against the state prevent citizens from acting upon the very definition of citizenship. If we want a new kind of democratic citizen, then we must reinvent the means by which democratic citizens are known and produced. This is not to say that revolution is out of the question, just that a revolutionary subject, like a democratic subject, must be made. That the techniques of Octavia Hill's COS were draconian does not decree that all techniques for making citizens must be Victorian. It is just as possible to produce sex radicals as to make good workers, to produce cyborgs rather than "useful" citizens. The rise of the social signaled a new scope for freedom as well as a new scope for power. The point is, citizens are always already subject to power even in the "free space" of civil society.

3

The Will to Empower: Technologies of Citizenship and the War on Poverty

"**E**mpowerment" emerged out of the 1960s as a strategy with near universal appeal, a strategy that links, but does not necessarily unite, the urban poor with feminists, ACT UP with civil rights movements, undocumented labor with gang truce organizers, welfare rights activists with environmentalists. Social movements and radical activists share little in the way of solidarity across the lines of race, class, gender, and sexuality, but they do share a method, a strategy for "empowerment." The political logic and techniques of empowerment developed in social programs and reform movements produced a technology of citizenship — a method for constituting citizens out of subjects and maximizing their political participation. Technologies of citizenship, such as those aimed at empowering "the poor,"[1] link the subjectivity of citizens to their subjection, and link activism to discipline.

⌐My argument here poses a challenge to the readiness with which we use "empowerment" to signify an unquestionably noble or radical political strategy.⌐My suspicions probably became a bit more widespread once Jack Kemp and Bill Clinton have equated "empowerment" with the privatization of public services and with market solutions to the problems of urban poverty and racism ("empowerment zones"). Since the 1980s the logic of empowerment has been mobilized as often by neoconservatives as by feminists and the left. Activist neoconservatives Jack Kemp and Richard Darman delight in "stealing one of the Left's words," aiming to "empower" the poor by allowing them to govern their own housing — or, in other words, by privatizing public housing projects. In Kemp's formulation, public housing residents could become self-governing, relieving the government of its obligation to govern.

The neoconservative variety of empowerment, in fact, takes on questions of legitimacy that heretofore preoccupied those on the left. Peter Berger and Richard Neuhaus, neoconservatives financed by the American Enterprise Institute for Public Policy Research, argue that neighborhood, family, church, and voluntary associations can be refashioned to mediate between citizen and state in a way that works to relegitimize a political order in crisis. "The proposal is that, if these institutions could be more imaginatively recognized in public policy, individuals would be more 'at home' in society, and the political order would be more 'meaningful.'"[2] The authors acknowledge that they derive their understanding of alienation from the Marxist tradition.

What is the relationship between neoconservative attempts at "empowering the poor" and the attempts to organize and mobilize the poor by the New Left and the antipoverty movements that began in the 1960s and continue to mobilize today?[3] Distinguishing the intentions of the left from those of the neo-conservatives is a simple matter: the left uses empowerment to generate political resistance; the right, to produce rational economic and entrepreneurial actors. Yet⌐the tactics for empowerment mobilized in innumerable programs — to help battered women, to fight red-lining, to fight gangs, to reform prostitutes, to govern public housing projects, prisons, and workfare (to name only a few) — share a political strategy: to act upon others by getting them to act in their own interest.⌐It is the content of powerless people's interests over which the right and the left disagree.

⌐From any ideological perspective, those interests must be constituted in order to be acted upon. The will to empower may be well intentioned, but it is a strategy for constituting and regulating the political subjectivities of the "empowered." Whether inspired by the market or by the promise of self-government and autonomy, the object of empowerment is to act upon another's interests and desires in order to conduct their actions toward an appropriate end; thus "empowerment" is itself a power relationship and one deserving of careful scrutiny.

The relationship between political power and the poor I am concerned with here does not reveal the forceful repression (visible or invisible) of the poor or their exclusion from politics, nor does it reveal their muted consent. Rather, I focus on the productive effects of power which promote, transform, and act upon the capacities of the poor. Technologies of citizenship are the means by which government works *through* rather than against the subjectivities of citizens. The logic of empowerment targets the capacities of the "powerless," measures and seeks to maximize their actions, motivations, interests, and economic and political involvements. Here power works by soliciting the active participation of the poor in dozens of programs on the local level, programs that aim at the transformation of the poor into self-sufficient, active, productive, and participatory citizens. The liberal arts of government, as I have been arguing, are actionable only on the condition that citizens carry out the purposes of government. Again, I do not mean the purposes of the state; "the poor" are governed, so to speak, but not strictly by *the* government or the state.

The history of the present will to empower can be traced back to the nineteenth-century reform movements discussed in previous chapters. More immediately, contemporary techniques and rationalities of empowerment can be traced back to the War on Poverty and the antipoverty movements of the 1960s. Empowerment is associated both with the innovations devised by Great Society reformers and with the New Left and civil rights emphases on self-government and community power. Although the War on Poverty failed to empower "the poor" permanently or to secure their solidarity, it did succeed in developing the strategy of empowerment as a solution to the problems of poverty. I offer not a new explanation of political apathy or powerlessness but a new look at how the conception of powerlessness was mobilized by radicals, reformers, and social scientists. I show how the antipoverty movement defined and constructed "the poor" as "powerless" and how social scientific knowledge of the poor was then tied to their "empowerment" and eventual self-government. The history of Community Action Programs (CAP)—just one episode in the history of the present will to empower—illustrates the intimate relationship between subjectivity and subjection which is embedded in technologies of citizenship, in efforts to combat poverty and powerlessness, and in strategies for empowering "the poor."

The Political Logic of Empowerment

Although subjectivity can be and all too often is brutally repressed, the operations of power which *promote* subjectivity are neither benign nor neutral. Critically examining the will to empower requires recognizing that despite the good, even radical, intentions of those who seek to empower others, relations of empowerment are in fact relations of power in and of themselves. The ordinary use of "empowerment" is illustrated in the following passage from Ann Bookman and Sandra Morgen in a book called *Women and the Politics of Empowerment*:

> We use the term empowerment to connote a spectrum of political activity ranging from acts of individual resistance to mass political mobilizations that challenge the basic power relations in our society. . . . For these women, empowerment begins when they change their ideas about the causes of their powerlessness, when they recognize the systemic forces that oppress them, and when they act to change the conditions of their lives.[4]

Note that the three parts to empowerment — consciousness, knowledge, action — connote the transition from powerlessness to full citizenship, from subjection to subjectivity.

First, it is typical of the logic of empowerment to dichotomize power and powerlessness. For example, Jacqueline Pope, a welfare rights activist and scholar, asserts that state intrusion destroys the capacities of African Americans to govern themselves: "These bureaucracies are responsible for blocking and defusing any restlessness or activities that might point towards a Black cultural reawakening, self-help, or political empowerment."[5] Pope argues that political participation would occur spontaneously were it not for the intrusion of the state and the colonization of black communities by public service bureaucracies. She carefully distinguishes her intentions for empowerment from the market-driven strategies of neoconservatives; rather than privatization, Pope seeks public and democratic control over public services. The problem and the strategy are the same, however: to limit government intervention by getting people to govern themselves.

According to Pope, black communities, once they are colonized, become "depoliticized," making it necessary for organizers, public programs and activists to refashion the poor into active citizens who are willing to hold public service providers accountable and capable of doing so. "Public assistance can grind away all semblance of dignity and self-worth, leaving its recipients to hate themselves and conclude, albeit falsely, that they have no alternatives to provide for themselves and their children."[6] The problem, then, is how to act upon the *subjective* self-understandings or the consciousness of citizens, and so to empower.

Second, just as the politics of empowerment on the left and right are not distinguishable by their tactics and targets, neither can they be adequately distinguished by claiming that the object of one is progressive political change and of the other, political conformity to the economic rationality of capitalism. At first glance, on the left empowerment is *political* empowerment, to be measured by political participation and political resistance. But it is important to recognize and call into question the exceptional status granted in the passage quoted above to relations of empowerment. The authors go on to argue that empowerment itself is not a power relationship but a "*process*," not a political-power relationship but "a *social* relationship" (my emphasis). This formulation of empowerment is typical in making the assumption that relations of empowerment are *not* relations of power, and not sites of resistance and participation in and of themselves. Yet how is the subjectivity of the "empowered" woman so transformed? How is it that the authors so clearly distinguish themselves from "these women"? Who infuses the powerless with power? And is that not an exercise of power? How is an "empowered" woman fabricated out of a "powerless" woman?

Third, empowerment is typically treated as a simple quantitative increase in the amount of power possessed by an individual. Technologies of citizenship — the organizer's "issue campaign," the radical's "revolutionary consciousness," the social worker's "plan for self-sufficiency," the social scientist's "theory of power," the neoconservative's "empowerment zone," the feminist's "self-esteem" — all seek to mobilize and maximize the subjectivities of those perceived to lack the power, hope, consciousness, and initiative to act on behalf of their own interests. Understood as a means of combatting exclusion and powerlessness, relations of empowerment are, in fact, akin to relations of government that both constitute and fundamentally transform the subject's capacity to act; rather than merely increasing that capacity, empowerment alters and shapes it. During the War on Poverty, "the poor" were not excluded by power from participating in the definition and provision of their own needs so much as they were transformed by that definition and provision. I work from the assumption, then, that the "powerless" do not exist as such prior to the application of technologies of citizenship; the "powerless" are the object and the outcome of the will to empower.

The object of my inquiry here is not empowerment per se, nor is it my intention to judge the will to empower as inevitably corrupt. The will to empower is *neither* clearly liberatory *nor* clearly repressive; rather, it is typical of the liberal arts of conduct and the political rationality of the welfare state. The focus here is on *relations* of empowerment, which include the following four characteristics.

First, empowerment is a relationship established by expertise, although expertise is constantly contested. Not only the expertise of the "experts" but also the expertise of the poor as the "real" experts on poverty, as well as the authority of representatives of subordinated groups — all are contested, routinely consulted, and documented. Second, it is a democratically unaccountable exercise of power in that the relationship is typically initiated by one party seeking to empower another. Third, it is dependent upon knowledge of those to be empowered, typically found in social scientific models of power or powerlessness and often gained through the self-description and self-disclosure of the subject to be empowered. The will to empower ourselves and others has spread across academic disciplines, social services, neighborhood agencies, social movements, and political groups, forging new relationships of power alongside new conceptualizations of power. Fourth, relations of empowerment are simultaneously voluntary *and* coercive — a point that is made clear below.

The Political Economy of Empowerment

What is meant by the "powerlessness" of the poor? What kind of power, exactly, leads to "empowerment"? What kind of power was distributed in the War on Poverty?

The history of Community Action Programs, although extremely short, tells much about how power (and empowerment) works in a democracy. In the hope of solving once and for all the problems of poverty and inequality in the American democratic system, the Johnson administration declared a War on Poverty. The Economic Opportunity Act of 1964 openly acknowledged the existence of persistent inequality in "the other America" and established several new programs to combat poverty and create opportunity: Job Corps, Head Start, work-study, neighborhood centers, and Volunteers in Service to America (VISTA). To coordinate and govern this range of new and existing services, the policy of "maximum feasible participation" was adopted, and CAPs quickly became the controversial centerpiece of the War on Poverty.[7]

The administration chose the strategy of redistributing power — not just money and jobs and child care, not just goods and services, but power. The War on Poverty was waged with the assumption that the powerlessness of the poor was the root cause of their poverty, not the actions of the powerful. Even the most radical thinkers, though they identified capitalist-class exploitation and racism as the causes of inequality, nonetheless traced poverty (as Jacqueline Pope does) to the (in)actions, (in)capacities, and powerlessness of the poor.

According to guidelines issued by the Office of Economic Opportunity (OEO), "The long range objective of every community action program is to effect a permanent increase in the capacity of individuals, groups, and communities afflicted by poverty to deal effectively with their own problems so that they need no further assistance. Poverty is a condition of need, helplessness and hopelessness."[8] Defined by all that they lacked, the poor needed help, but it was to be given in the form of a stimulus to act for themselves. In the model of powerlessness operationalized in antipoverty programs, power was clearly intended to work through, not against, the subjectivity of the poor.

During the War on Poverty the powerlessness of the poor was posited not as an objective fact, but as a subjective "sense of powerlessness." CAP legislation acknowledged the objective causes of poverty — low wages, racism, unemployment, lack of child care — and the War on Poverty devised several programs to ameliorate the objective circumstances of the poor. But the subjective causes of powerlessness became the object of intense governmentalization in these programs, primarily because the poor often chose not to participate and failed to constitute themselves as a constituency for antipoverty policy. Their "apathy" and political inaction became the central target of programs and was posited as the most significant cause of poverty and later the cause of the failure of those programs.

George Brager, director of the militant Mobilization for Youth, a program for the prevention of juvenile delinquency that was adapted as a model for CAPs, asserted that the object of reform must be the subjectivities of the poor: "We believe the personal sense of powerlessness felt by low income people is a major cause of their isolation and apathy. . . . To encourage education and social learning, therefore, it is necessary to decrease the sense of powerlessness."[9] Presumably, youth were so beaten down by poverty, racism, and inequality that a kind of hopelessness was the real cause of poverty. The evidence for their "apathy" was found in their refusal to help themselves and act in their own interest by joining the Ford Foundation's antidelinquency effort.

The subjectivities of youth were made into objects of an extraordinary research and programmatic effort that was adopted later as the strategy to win the War on Poverty.[10] If delinquent youth and the poor in general simply were not willing to participate in voluntary programs, the first requirement was to get them to take an interest in their own empowerment. Reformers had to face the problem of "drawing people into the planning of their own welfare."[11] In a 1962 prospectus for CAP funds, a New Haven grant application asserted:

> The city is the people. New jobs can be provided but some people are unwilling or afraid to apply for them. New housing projects can be built but some tenants will turn them into slums. New community centers can be opened but only a few people may choose to use them. Exciting educational programmes can be conceived but the people can let them die for lack of participation. Therefore, attention must be paid to the underlying motivations, attitudes, and values of the people of the city.[12]

In confronting the unwillingness of poor citizens to engage in reform efforts, even those efforts aimed at improving the lives of the poor themselves, reformers came up against the limit of democratic government. The government could not govern and could not win the War on Poverty without the voluntary participation of the poor.

The limit of democratic government was stretched by turning the empowerment and participation of the poor, the stimulation and exercise of their subjectivity, into the object of governmentalization and intervention. The will to empower, or the desire to help the poor, had to be balanced against the imperative that the poor must help themselves. The subjectivity of the poor had to be balanced with their subjection. The goal became to align the will to empower with the interests of the poor.

As Peter Bachrach and others summarized, "cooptative participation" is "an effective means of rehabilitating groups of persons who lack the knowledge or the built-in desire to help themselves." The limit of democratic government was to be overcome by transforming the poor into a constituency for antipoverty programs. "The critical question . . . is whether the programs can engender among the poor a sense of vested interest in the programs and a growing preparedness to organize and struggle for the introduction, improvement, and enlargement of anti-poverty projects."[13] This is to say not that no subjectivity exists at all prior to government but that the will to empower depends upon combining the capacities of the unemployed, juveniles, and single mothers by turning them into one political constituency.

Explicitly citing the nonparticipation of the poor, CAP legislation established the purpose of "maximum feasible participation" as

> the development and implementation of all programs and projects designed to serve the poor or low-income areas with the maximum feasible participation of residents of the areas and members of the groups served, so as to best stimulate and take full advantage of capabilities for self-advancement and assure that those programs and projects are otherwise meaningful to and widely utilized by their intended beneficiaries.[14]

In CAPs, the balance between "helping" the poor and the poor "helping themselves" was a delicate one and the subject of much criticism and debate.[15] The participation of the poor was a key planning problem. Attempts were made to "solicit" and to "motivate." Special committees were suggested "to focus attention on problems and methods of involving the hard-to-reach poor and to evaluate the effectiveness of the approaches adopted."[16]

Peter Marris and Martin Rein, whose *Dilemmas of Social Reform* stands as one of the best accounts of the War on Poverty, quote the following from a juvenile delinquency program guideline: "When specific goals are predetermined, the project must face that actual danger or the charge of manipulation of people. When goals are not predetermined, the project must face the problem of lack of control and unanticipated directions, with which the project may have difficulty living."[17] To balance the subjectivity of citizens with their subjection required an innovation in political rationality. Only certain innovations in democratic reform make it possible to overcome the obstacles that nonparticipation places in the path of governmentalization.

During the War on Poverty at least three innovations surfaced. First, "the poor" were isolated as a target of government intervention and their capacities calculated and inscribed into a policy for their "empowerment." Second, CAP set out to create a "community" for action by legislating the decentralization of power relationships and the multiplication of power relations between constituencies — the poor and juvenile delinquents, social scientists, social service vendors, the executive branch of government — which otherwise could not exercise power on one another. (Note that this is much the same as the goal set by recent efforts to reform the police in "community policing.") Third, professional reformers emerged as the instruments for applying technologies of citizenship and new theories of power and powerlessness.

I hasten to add that positing the powerlessness and apathy of the poor was not simply a justification for an otherwise illegitimate government intervention. Even those who were extremely suspicious of government intervention among the poor — those who favored revolutionary action over democratic reform, radicals such as Tom Hayden, who understood CAP as "serving chiefly to sharpen the capacity of the system for manipulation and oppression"[18] — regarded the subjectivities of the poor as obstructions in the way of radical political involvement.[19] As Hayden wrote in *Dissent*: "There can be no poor people's movement in any form unless the poor can overcome their fear and embarrassment. . . . All this means fostering in everyone that sense of decision-making power which American society works to destroy. Only in this way can a movement be built which the Establishment can neither buy off nor manage, a movement too vital ever to become a small clique of spokesmen."[20] The lack of a sense of decision-making power, in this radical formulation, kept the poor from organizing politically on their own behalf and according to their own interests. The "apathy" of the poor was for the New Left, as it was for liberal reformers, the central and continuing cause of their poverty and unequal status. The key to revolution and reform alike was understood to be in the independent and voluntary participation of the poor in their own emancipation.

Modeling the Poor

How did "the poor" become a group with a shared set of problems and interests? How did "the poor" become an object of governmental policy? Why were people willing to define themselves and organize around being "poor" rather than or in addition to race and class?[21] To motivate "the poor" to help themselves, they had to be known; however, the truth of the poor could not be told before the poor were isolated as a group.[22] Part of telling the truth of the poor (especially the part that the poor were to tell about themselves) was precisely to constitute the poor as a group by defining their characteristics, capacities, and desires. During the War on Poverty the disparate and diverse peoples that came to occupy the category of "the poor" were transformed into a calculable, knowable grouping and made available for government by forming a category that, as Nikolas Rose puts it, "could be used in political arguments and administrative decisions."[23]

The category of "the poor" was reintroduced as if it were a new and shocking discovery within a political context deeply divided by region, gender, race and class. It was a category (re)invented to cross social and geographic divisions, such as urban and rural, and to include Appalachian coal miners, black urban single-parent families, the working poor, juvenile delinquents, alcoholics, and the elderly, among others. Moreover, the political context was one shaped by the civil rights movement, and free speech and antiwar protests. Michael Harrington, a socialist from the Catholic Worker movement, did more than anyone, perhaps, to identify and isolating the poor as a group and define their subjectivity. Harrington, whose best-selling book *The Other America* is credited with spurring the War on Poverty, argued that all the poor shared a culture: "Perhaps the most important analytic point to have emerged in this description of the other America is the fact that poverty in America forms a culture, a way of life and feeling, that makes it whole." [24] A subjectivity was thus posited for "the Other America" on the basis of the "culture of poverty" thesis. [25]

The notion that the poor share a culture helped create an administrative category of policy analysis out of a vast assortment of divided people whose defining characteristic was said to be their subjective sense of powerlessness. Harrington wrote, "In a sense, one might define the contemporary poor in the United States as those who, for reasons beyond their control, cannot help themselves." [26] The fact that the poor were not mobilized politically in their own interest was the rationale behind planning and program design in the War on Poverty. In sum, the demographic model of the poor was based upon their lack of political participation, lack of shared interest, and lack of motivation to solve the problems—their own problems—of poverty.

A crucial part of knowing the poor was knowing what the poor wanted and how they defined the needs and conditions of poverty. Sargent Shriver, director of OEO, argued that the components of CAP—"education and training, experience and motivation, confidence and health, hope and self-reliance"—were not reaching the poor because program designers did not engage the poor themselves in defining their own needs. "It isn't reaching the consumer—the poor themselves. And so, we have to engage in a new kind of market research. We have to find out why the old product didn't appeal to the consumer—to one-fifth of the market. And only the poor—the consumer—can tell us." [27] The market research and consumer analogy is still a bit misleading because, as Shriver so often pointed out, the poor themselves have to be engaged not just in consuming the programs of the state but in stating their interests and desires as individuals and communities willing to engage in the antipoverty effort. Establishing the expertise of the poor set a standard for including them in planning efforts — or, in one of the antipoverty era's most popular phrases, "planning with and not for the poor."

CAPs operated according to a political rationality geared to a calculated, evaluated, and supervised "maximization" of the energies of the poor. The willingness and the capacity of "the poor" to act in their own interest, then, became the object of intense research, intervention, and governmentalization. Even though the poor were divided by race, for example, their differences added up to inclusion in the "other America," a single unit of administration and policy debate. Harrington went on to advocate an all-out assault on the culture of poverty. A campaign against poverty "should think, not in terms of this or that aspect of poverty, but along the lines of establishing new communities, of substituting a human environment for the inhuman one that now exists." [28] Harrington reinvented "the poor" as a group of people who could be acted upon and who could become "human" themselves only by acting together to form "communities."

Harrington sought to mobilize the poor on their own behalf, to maximize their participation in the welfare state. The goal of "maximum feasible participation" in CAPs was not for the poor to constitute antipoverty programs, but for the poor to be constituted as a group with interests and the desire to act upon those interests. Others seeking a "political awakening among the poverty population" argued that "the over-riding issue is not whether participation of the poor contributes to the effectiveness of antipoverty programs. The critical question, rather, is whether the programs can engender among the poor a sense of vested interest in the programs and a growing preparedness to organize and struggle for the introduction, improvement, and enlargement of anti-poverty projects." [29]

Without actually initiating the actions of the poor or inhibiting their freedom, anti-poverty programs stimulated the poor to act in concert as a constituency. Reformers sought a strategy "that would transmute the institutionalized expression of a common purpose into *ungoverned* personal action," and found it in Community Action. [30] In short, modeling the poor, so to speak, was an essential aspect of government.

Community Action agencies were clearly designed to govern and administer the War on Poverty but were also, in and of themselves, distinct governmental domains or small publics established "by and for the poor."

Though intended to be a public arena for the government of the poor, CAPs were publics not directed by the government but by the voluntary cooperation of all the public and private actors involved in the "local coalition" fighting the War on Poverty.[31] According to the OEO, "It is a process of building bridges between the poor and non-poor, between government officials and private groups, between professionals and laymen, between agencies which operate related programs, between the poor and the opportunities which could help them become self-sufficient, productive, respected citizens. Of great importance is the building of bridges between one poor person and another, so they can share the dignity of self-help in escaping from poverty."[32]

Notice that even the relationships between poor people themselves were to be matters of organization and government; no ties were left untouched. "Self-help" did not mean that autonomous selves got together to help one another. Rather, self-help meant that the government intervened to create relations of help between selves. Even though the poor presumably shared a culture of poverty, ties between the poor had to be fabricated and were to be the outcome of government intervention. The poor were to indicate their own needs and the causes of their impoverishment; in doing so, it was hoped, they would enlist themselves in meeting those needs.

The terrain of government established in CAP legislation was, of course, the "community," a set of relationships (or "bridges") legislated into existence to link the poor to programs, experts, agencies, and government. In effect, relations of government were established outside the government in "local" relationships. CAPs did not avoid the imposition of government but extended government into new terrains by "maximizing" the participation of the poor. CAP legislation created multiple publics and decentralized decision-making over what shape the antipoverty effort would take.

According to Marris and Rein, however, the delegation of power caused an explosion of conflict that led directly to the rapid failure of the CAPs. They had no clear constituency, and the "community" established by legislation never materialized, in part because social scientists, local political elites, and "the poor" were deeply divided over purpose: "The agency was, in effect, trying to impose its own resolution of the rival claims of expert knowledge, political manoeuvre and the self-assertion of the poor to determine the direction of social policy."[33] The "community" of community action was never adequately constituted or, rather, never adequately brought to some common purpose. "As a quasi-public nonprofit corporation," Ralph Kramer explained, "the CAPs were in a no-man's-land of legitimacy. They needed a constituency for political reasons but were constrained in the development of one by the diverse character of their target populations, their limited resources and organizational capabilities, and their social service preoccupations."[34]

Part of the failure of CAP was surely in failing to unite a "community" divided by race, class, expertise, and interests. Mayors were soon storming Washington in protest against CAPs, and members of Congress were charging CAP organizers with agitating, demonstrating, and otherwise radically threatening the very government that paid their salaries. Sargent Shriver, head of the OEO, was attacked publicly by his own constituency. Although a few of the antipoverty programs devised by the Great Society continue to operate — most notably Head Start and work-study — the life span of CAPs was short and extremely rocky. By 1967 support was waning, and by 1969 federal funding for the "maximum feasible participation" of the poor in the War on Poverty had been pulled.

Still, CAP did not fail so much as it succeeded in creating a logic of empowerment and a model for overcoming or stretching the limits of democratic government. The logic of empowerment went well beyond interest-group pluralism by extending and decentralizing relations of government to terrains beyond the state or formal governmental apparatus, and those relationships have lasted well beyond the demise of CAP. Moreover, conflict should not be taken for program failure. Relationships of power depend upon the instability created by conflict between power and resistance; in the case of CAPs, great care was taken to avoid helping the poor directly because that would be to make the poor "dependent." Again, the subjection of the poor had to be balanced against their subjectivity. As Foucault noted, "It would not be possible for power relations to exist without points of insubordination which, by definition, are means of escape."[35] The limits of democratic government were tested in the War on Poverty in a way quite possibly unprecedented, for the agency that was granted to street-level bureaucrats, activists, and radicals at every point threatened to and often did boil over into full-blown rebellion.

Government did not strive to repress the rival demands of the civil rights movement, the anti-war movement, the experts, and the poor but linked those demands — especially for the redistribution of power — to the governing relationships established at the local level. Relations of government multiplied — between "the poor" and programs, "poor" people and other "poor" people, "the poor" and their supposed "community," the poor person and him- or herself. According to Kramer,

> There is probably no turning back, even though there may not be any continuing mandate or sanction from OEO for the participation of the poor. The idea is now abroad and has become linked with the growing demands for Black Power or "Brown Power." . . . there is now an informed constituency of former nonprofessionals and participants, supportive caretakers, and ethnic minority leaders who can be expected to invoke precedent and exert pressure to sustain planning *with* and not *for* the poor.[36]

The precedent was set for the poor themselves to influence planning and programs and to participate in decision-making. A link was established between effective government and the self-government of the poor as a means of overcoming the limits of democratic reform.

Operationalizing Power

In 1966, political scientist and pluralist Grant McConnell stated a principle and limit of democratic reform: "Since there are too many people to address individually, they must all get together in their own associations and agree — voluntarily. Then government could put its stamp upon their informal, cooperative, and free decisions. Government would thus have achieved the purpose of a free people, and without coercion."[37] McConnell recognized that liberal democratic government worked best when it worked through, rather than against, the subjectivities of citizens.

There is an obvious resonance between the pluralist view of government and power and Michel Foucault's conceptions of power and governmentality: both Foucault and the pluralists argue that power is plural; however, the similarities end there.[38] According to the pluralist view, relations of governance are based on *either* voluntary consent *or* coercion; government operates either through the voluntary and autonomous subjectivity of citizens or through the coercion and repression of their subjectivity. The pluralists, like the feminists I cited earlier, dichotomize and juxtapose power and powerlessness, subjectivity and subjection, coercion and consent, as opposite effects of government. Foucault's view of power allows us to see that subjectivity and subjection, like citizens and subjects, are never so clearly distinguished in liberal democratic societies.

Foucault's conception of governmentality allows us to see further that in order to create a relationship of power and the possibility for governance, two requirements must be met: "That the 'other' (the one over whom power is exercised) be thoroughly recognized and maintained to the very end as a person who acts; and that, faced with a relationship of power, a whole field of responses, reactions, results, and possible inventions may open up."[39] The "others" in this case are the poor who were defined (on both the left and the right) at the outset as those who do not act, who are apathetic, and who understand themselves to be powerless. Without the empowerment of the poor it would not be possible to act upon their actions or to extend relations of power and government to them. Hence, the distribution of power and the maximization of participation became the cornerstones of antipoverty policy. Before "the poor" could be engaged and acted upon, they had first to be armed, to be constituted as an army, a single unit.

McConnell assumed that the government acts when the people do, out of some kind of organic and shared interest developed in an ungoverned sphere of civil society. The pluralist view fails to account for the fact that when people do *not* get together in their own associations, or at least when there is the perception that the poor are apathetic, governmental interventions are designed to create the possibility for people to come together. To govern, then, means first to stir up the desire, the interest, and the will to participate or act politically. Establishing a relationship of governance requires first reconstituting the poor and powerless as acting subjects. In short, according to the logic of empowerment, the poor must be made to act.

By way of contrast, many people were far less concerned with the apathy and inaction of the poor than with the mobilization of the poor: the potential for violence, black nationalism, civil rights, student activism, and other perceived threats to the established white power structure. As discussed in the preceding chapter, Samuel Huntington believed "democratic distemper" was a very real threat to democratic order. How was it possible during this unprecedented mobilization to posit the "powerlessness" of the poor?

Nevertheless the measurement of nonparticipation became a key to the planning process for combatting poverty. Peter Bachrach and Morton Baratz, social scientists actively engaged in Community Action Programs, operationalized and measured the "second face of power" in terms of actions and events that did *not* happen: "nonparticipation," "non-events," and "non-decisions."[40] Again, and most significantly, the focus of research was on nonparticipation specifically because the poor were not participating in programs designed to combat poverty. The measurement was applied in a predictably selective manner only to those whose participation was sought in reform programs: for example, white middle-class women's lack of power and participation was not an object of planning.

As I illustrated in Chapter 1, radical scholars explained power and powerlessness in terms of the exclusion of the poor through non-actions and non-decisions, as well as in terms of the ideological manipulation of the poor against their real interests.[41] What is less well documented is the fact that political scientists who were concerned with finding a way to make the actions of the powerful visible and accountable actually helped to invent and operationalize new means for acting upon the subjectivities of the poor. In their reflections on power, political scientists exhibited the will to empower, to know and to mobilize the poor according to the policies and logic of empowerment. Social scientific theories of power linked the distribution and decentralization of power with maximized participation, which linked the subjectivities of the poor to their subjection — albeit their self-subjection as self-governing subjects.

To counter pluralist claims that nonparticipation signaled consent rather than powerlessness, as well as to explain the absence of political conflict in the face of blatant inequality, social scientists theorized the relationship between nonparticipation and powerlessness. Radical scholars sought to uncover the submerged means of manipulation used to repress conflict and to exclude the political participation of the poor. In fact, the (non)participation of the poor became as much a question of social scientific method as it was a question of poverty and politics.

Bachrach and Baratz set out to measure the effectiveness of CAPs in "maximizing participation." They needed measurements and evaluations of participation, but the problem was a *lack* of participation. What they devised, then, were methods for measuring and evaluating nonparticipation and powerlessness. According to the logic of empowerment, nonparticipation was taken to indicate a power relationship. The social scientific operationalization of power was, so to speak, a means of putting power into action.

I have already shown that the participation and constitution of "the poor" was a means of overcoming the limits of democratic reform. For the purpose of "empowering" the poor to participate, power was redistributed through CAPs, and new arenas ("communities") for the exercise of power were established by decentralizing power and extending relations of government into new domains. The third innovation of CAP was devised to balance the enhanced subjectivity of the poor with their subjection.

Arming the Poor

Someone had to apply the technologies of citizenship and new theories of power generated in the War on Poverty, someone whose expertise lay in spurring others into action. "Of all the innovations of community action," as Marris and Rein assessed it, "this may prove the most important: it created the professional reformer, and invented an organizational framework appropriate to his function."[42] It is important to note that the professional organizer-reformer was not an entirely new character; there were historical precedents. In the American context, think of Frederick Douglass, Jane Addams, Saul Alinsky, and public works projects such as the Tennessee Valley Authority. The innovation during the War on Poverty, however, was in the particular constellation of expertise, activism, and theories of power. What made CAP organizers unique was the link they provided between "helping" the poor and "self-help" on the national level.

According to the logic of empowerment, though, the social scientist or organizer must exempt him- or herself from the exercise of power. The poor themselves were to take over the function of evaluating and experimenting in programs designed to "maximize" participation, as Bachrach, Baratz, and Margaret Levi explained:

> If effective inroads on the poverty problem are to be made, experts in the field must — at least during the formative period — possess sufficient powers of manipulation to control the situation, in order to select the range of "suitable" policy options and to allow for experimentation and innovation (within certain prescribed boundaries). The experts' ultimate objective, however, must be to make themselves superfluous, vacating in favor of leaders indigenous to the participant groups.[43]

Social scientists and program organizers were to govern at a distance, but ultimately, government was to become self-government, making the social reformer "superfluous." In other words, the job of government was clearly delegated to the experts, who were to use their knowledge and their powers to experiment and constantly evaluate the process of redistributing power while simultaneously attempting to solicit the participation of the poor. The actions and subjectivities of the poor would, it was hoped, be brought in line with a certain model of power and empowerment. The claim to knowing the poor — including the claims made by the poor to knowing themselves, their own needs and desires — was tied to a technology for their "empowerment" and the maximization of political participation.]

Once again, the relationship of power between the helper and the helped in the liberal arts of government is displaced. Hayden's "radical" organizer, for example, exhibits what I call the will to empower by displacing the will and the power of the organizer:

> What is required is a certain kind of organizing that tries to make people understand their own worth and dignity. This work depends on the existence of "material issues" as a fundamental organizing point — high rents, voting rights, unpaved roads, and so on — but it moves from there into the ways such issues are related to personal life. The organizer spends hours and hours in the community, listening to people, drawing out their own ideas, rejecting their tendency to depend on him for solutions.[44]

The plan to have the function of the organizer taken over by the poor was made a part of CAP legislation, which explicitly restricted the political participation of those program directors and organizers who were on the federal payroll. Professional organizers, strictly excluded from political life, were left with the need to constitute others as the constituency for their programs. Empowerment was planned to become, effortlessly, "self-empowerment." Expert reformers, private foundations, voluntary associations were and continue to be nongovernmental means of government.

The Subjects of Power

By emphasizing the productive aspects of power, I do not wish to disregard the degree to which political power blatantly and too often displays itself through gross domination and overt force. But when it does so, we have no difficulty identifying its presence. For example, during the 1960s and the War on Poverty, the FBI and the National Guard were mobilized to repress the expression and organization of dissent by antiwar protesters and the Black Panthers, in civil rights demonstrations and urban race riots. Overt repression and state violence were visible (though often planned and conducted in secret) on the nightly news and oddly juxtaposed to the escalating violence in Vietnam. More recently, repressive measures have been visible in the mobilization of police and the National Guard in south central Los Angeles, in the unprecedented rates of incarceration and increases in the executions of prisoners, as well as the treatment of immigrants. Even in more subtle forms of repression — police ticketing the homeless for sleeping in public places, for example, or the relentless exploitation by vice police of poor women and drug addicts — we can easily identify power in its repressive form.

The popular thesis on the left that CAPs were invented by the government primarily to divert, co-opt, repress, and undermine legitimate opposition to the state assumes that "the poor" do indeed have objective interests that can be co-opted.[45] I have shown that "the poor" cannot have interests of their own until and unless they are constituted as a group. That did not happen until the War on Poverty was waged; government did not repress the poor but invented the poor as a group with interests and powers. Before governmental intervention — and I mean that in the broadest sense — "the poor" were disparate, isolated, and often in conflict with one another; they were Appalachian coal miners, urban single mothers, illiterates, unskilled black migrants from the South, southern fundamentalists, the elderly, "delinquent" youths, and the unemployed. The assumption that people do not know their own best interests is politically suspect, but that their interests do not divide them as much as they promise to unite them is unfounded. Nevertheless, the implicit elitism of the will to empower, claiming to know what is best for others, does not condemn it to failure or necessarily to a reactionary status. Empowerment is a power relationship, a relationship of government; it can be used well or badly.

My account differs from other critical accounts of the War on Poverty because I insist that it was not aimed at demobilizing the poor in a time of upheaval or at repressing and co-opting radical civil rights and student activists. To the contrary, I argue that CAPs created rather than quelled conflict. The War on Poverty was no misnomer — it sought to generate and win a confrontation with the urban poor — but the legislation that declared it did not command any troops. The War on Poverty (like other wars in recent memory) had first to arm the enemy in order to engage in conflict. In other words, the exercise of power in the War on Poverty did not determine the actions of the poor but determined that the poor would act.

4

Revolutions Within:
Self-Government and Self-Esteem

What breach of order is it possible to commit in solitude?

GUSTAVE DE BEAUMONT AND ALEXIS DE TOCQUEVILLE

Some feminists have criticized Gloria Steinem's best-seller *Revolution from Within: A Book of Self-Esteem* for calling a feminist retreat to personal life from the collective political front.[1] Deidre English's reservations are typical: "What is disturbing is to see the empowering therapy supplant the cause. The strategic vision of social revolution here has all but been replaced with a model of personal recovery."[2] Echoing Tocqueville, critics ask how it is possible to challenge the existing order from a solitary position. I return to Tocqueville's question later on, after I explain how the self-esteem movement associates the self and the social order in what Tocqueville himself might have called a "science of association." Is it possible to wage a real "revolution from within"? Critics are afraid that feminism is going the way of Steinem's self-esteem movement and trading in collective action and confrontation for the solitude of self-reflection, exchanging the political for the personal.

English assumes that "real" politics does not occur in personal life and that genuine political resistance is aimed at the social order as a whole, not at one's self. Reading the self-esteem movement as a symptom of the political demobilization of feminism, critics charge that movement with taking the slogan "the personal is political" a bit too literally. To the contrary, I argue in this chapter that critics should take the slogan quite literally in order to recognize the ways in which the political has been reconstituted at the level of the self. The self-esteem movement does not so much avoid "real" political problems as transform the level on which it is possible to address those problems.

Further, I argue there is little that is personal about self-esteem.[3] In fact, what is remarkable and of political importance about Steinem's book is not where she directs her revolutionary subjectivity — to the personal or the political fronts — but that she turns self-esteem into a social relationship and a political obligation. The self-esteem movement is not merely a misbegotten strategy for women's liberation, as Steinem's critics charge; it is more than that. It is a movement that does not leave politics and power as they were but seeks to constitute a "state of esteem," a new political order, and a new set of social relations.

The self-esteem movement was spearheaded in 1983 by the California Task Force to Promote Self-Esteem and Personal and Social Responsibility. The Task Force promised to deliver programs (what I have been calling technologies of citizenship) that could solve social problems — from crime and poverty to gender inequality — by waging a social revolution not against capitalism, racism, and inequality, but against the order of the self and the way we govern our selves.

Steinem's best-selling book is only a small part of the self-esteem movement; it involves a whole range of experts, policy and social service professionals, and grass-roots activists. California Assembly Bill 3659, which established the Task Force, states that today's social problems have become ungovernable and seriously threaten democratic stability.[4] "Government and experts cannot fix these problems for us. It is only when each of us recognizes our individual personal and social responsibility to be part of the solution that we also realize higher 'self-esteem.'"[5] This is a social movement premised upon the limits of politics and the welfare state, the failures of American democracy, and the inability of government to control conflict; it is a "revolutionary" movement seeking to forge a new terrain of politics and a new mode of governing the self, not a new government. In short, in the discourse of self-esteem, the question of governance is a question of self-governance.

Liberation Therapy

Personal fulfillment becomes a social obligation in the discourse of self-esteem, an innovation that transforms the relationship of self-to-self into a relationship that is governable.[6] Self-fulfillment is no longer a personal or private goal. According to advocates, taking up the goal of self-esteem is something we owe to society, something that will defray the costs of social problems, something that will create a "true" democracy. Hence, the solution to the current "crisis of governability" is discovered in the capacity of citizens to act upon themselves, guided by the expertise of the social sciences and social service professionals.

A key finding reported by the California Task Force is that "self-esteem is the likeliest candidate for a *social vaccine*, something that empowers us to live responsibly and that inoculates us against the lures of crime, violence, substance abuse, teen pregnancy, child abuse, chronic welfare dependency, and educational failure. The lack of self-esteem is central to most personal and social ills plaguing our state and nation as we approach the end of the twentieth century."[7] More than a simple shot in the arm, self-esteem is a kind of "liberation therapy" that requires a complete reorientation to social problem-solving, as well as the mobilization of "every Californian" in an effort compared by advocates to the landing on the moon and the discovery of the atom.[8] Those scientific innovations carried the burden of social stability, but the new science of the self places the hope of liberation in the psychological state of the people, especially poor urban people of color to whom most of the "social ills" listed above are attributed.

Self-esteem is a practical technology for the production of certain kinds of selves — for "making up people," as Ian Hacking put it.[9] Self-esteem is a technology in the sense that it is a specialized knowledge of how to esteem our selves, how to estimate, calculate, measure, evaluate, discipline, and judge our selves. It is especially, though not exclusively, a literary technology: "self" emerges out of confrontation with texts, primarily, or with the telling and writing of personal narratives — a practice Steinem refers to as "bibliotherapy." We can learn and perform "bibliotherapy" upon ourselves or join any of the numerous agencies, associations, and programs set up to "enhance" self-esteem which have been catalogued, along with books and scholarly articles, by the California Task Force and in Steinem's book; compiling research is tantamount to delivering therapy.

One of the goals of the self-esteem movement is to elicit the participation of as many people as possible, and that means hearing their stories of struggle with their lack of self-esteem. Former California legislator John Vasconcellos claims that his efforts to establish the California Task Force to Promote Self-Esteem and Personal and Social Responsibility grew out of his own "personal struggle despite repeated successes and achievements in my life — to develop my own self-esteem," and that his commitment to building self-esteem came from his experience with the state's budget that spent "too little, too late [on] efforts to confine and/or repair our fellow Californians, whose lives are in distress and disrepair."[10] Similarly, Steinem ascribes her own lack of self-esteem to her role in the feminist movement and links her commitment to self-esteem to the limitations of political action.

Self-esteem program goals include getting clients to write and tell their personal narratives with an eye to the social good. Narratives bring people to see that the details of their private lives and their chances for improving their lives are inextricably linked to what is good for all of society. Steinem suggests that enlisting teenage girls, for example, to write down their personal narratives and their feelings about teenage pregnancy can result in the prevention of teenage pregnancy.[11] In the process of writing their personal narratives, the girls construct a self to act upon and to govern.

Working toward self-esteem is a way to subject citizens in the sense of making them "prone to" or "subject to" taking up the goals of self-esteem for themselves and their vision of the good society. We make our selves governable by taking up the social goal of self-esteem — just one minor example of what Foucault called "technologies of the self." As he described it, "through some political technology of individuals, we have been led to recognize ourselves as a society, as a part of a social entity, as part of a nation or of a state."[12] Transparency is established between the individual's goal of achieving self-esteem and the social goal of eliminating child abuse, crime, and welfare dependence. Those who undergo "revolution from within" are citizens doing the right thing; they join programs, they volunteer, but most important, they work on and improve their self-image. At all times, self-esteem calls upon individuals to act, to participate. "The continuation and future success of our democratic system of government and society are dependent upon the exercise of responsible citizenship by each and every Californian."[13]

Our relationship to our selves is directly related to citizenship because, by definition, "being a responsible citizen depends on developing personal and social responsibility."[14] One must accept the responsibility to subject one's self, to establish voluntarily a relationship between one's self and a tutelary power (such as a therapist or a social worker) and a technique of power (in a social program or a parenting class). Building self-esteem is a technology of citizenship and self-government for evaluating and acting upon our selves so that the police, the guards and the doctors do not have to. Consent in this case does not mean that there is no exercise of power; by isolating a self to act upon, to appreciate and to esteem, we avail ourselves of a terrain of action; we exercise power upon ourselves.

Society needs protection from those who lack self-esteem, according to advocates. Those who have failed to link their personal fulfillment to social reform are lumped together as "social problems," diagnosed as "lacking self-esteem," and charged with "antisocial behavior." Social scientists, as the foremost experts on the needs of society, along with social workers and other professionals such as philanthropists, policy experts, public health professionals, and politicians speak in the name of society's interests. Tutelary power is held by all those who speak for the interests and concerns of society at large; for example, *The Social Importance of Self-Esteem* is a volume dedicated to promoting the well-being of society.[15] Yet that power can be put into effect only by getting others to act.

I do not mean to underestimate the blatantly coercive and punitive measures taken by legislators, social workers, and other professionals under the guise of liberation therapy. Battered women are often coerced by the courts into participating in therapeutic programs that aim at their empowerment or self-esteem. Mothers caught up in the juvenile court system can be made to "graduate" from parenting courses, group therapies, and the like before the custody of their children is secure. The institution of foster care is easily made into a coercive apparatus for preparing mothers to become the kind of mothers deemed appropriate by society, by legislation, by philanthropists: the threat of taking children away is a primary tool of coercion.

But just as often, women are persuaded to participate in their own "empowerment" without threats. Governance in this case is something we do to our selves, not something done to us by those in power.[16] I am suggesting that we have wildly underestimated the extent to which *we are already self-governing*. Democratic government, even self-government, depends upon the ability of citizens to recognize, isolate, and act upon their own subjectivity, to be governors of their own selves. The ability of a citizen to generate a politically able self depends upon technologies of subjectivity and citizenship which link personal goals and desires to social order and stability, linking power to subjectivity.[17] The line between subjectivity and subjection is crossed when I subject my self, when I align my personal goals with those set out by reformers — both expert and activist — according to some notion of the social good. The norm of self-esteem links subjectivity to power; in the words of Nikolas Rose, it "binds subjects to a subjection that is the more profound because it appears to emanate from our autonomous quest for ourselves, it appears as a matter of our freedom."[18]

The call for self-government and democracy is extended beyond political institutions and economic relations by the self-esteem movement; the political goals of participation, empowerment, and collective action are extended to the terrain of the self. Steinem inverts the feminist slogan, "the personal is political" by claiming that "the political is personal." Nikolas Rose has shown how contemporary political technologies (such as efforts to achieve self-esteem) promise a certain kind of freedom, not offering "liberation from social constraints but rendering psychological constraints on autonomy conscious, and hence amenable to rational transformation. Achieving freedom becomes a matter not of slogans nor of political revolution, but of slow, painstaking, and detailed work on our own subjective and personal realities, guided by an expert knowledge of the psyche."[19]

The liberation promised by self-esteem originates within the relation of self-to-self but is not limited to the self. Indeed, self-esteem is advocated as a basis for the democratic development of the individual *and* society; it outlines a whole new set of social relationships and strategies for their development under the expert tutelage of "liberation therapists."

Constituting a State of Esteem

The California Task Force to Promote Self-Esteem and Personal and Social Responsibility was charged by the state legislature with compiling existing research on the relationship between "self-esteem" and six social problems: "chronic welfare dependence," alcoholism and drug abuse, crime and violence, academic failure, teenage pregnancy, and child abuse. Neil Smelser, a sociologist and a member of the Task Force, admits the failure of social scientists to identify the lack of self-esteem as the cause of social problems: "The news most consistently reported . . . is that the associations between self-esteem and its expected consequences are mixed, insignificant, or absent."[20] Yet despite the "disappointing" correlation found between the lack of self-esteem and the social problems listed,[21] the Task Force forged ahead, calling for increased funding for further research. Its members and the social scientists involved did not diagnose, empirically discover, or even describe an already existing malaise and its cure. Instead, they applied methods to measure what was not there: the focus of research moved to the *lack* of self-esteem and its (non)relation to social problems.

The Task Force in its final report quoted Professor Covington, who claims that self-esteem "challenges us to be more fully human. In addition to being an object of scientific investigation and also an explanation for behavior, self-esteem is above all a metaphor, a symbol filled with excess meaning that can ignite visions of what we as a people might become."[22]

From the "discovery" of its absence, social scientists have a created a tangible vision of a "state of esteem." Here the social sciences can be seen as productive sciences; the knowledge, measurements, and data they produce are constitutive of relations of governance as well as of the subjectivity of citizens. In devising the methods for measuring, evaluating, and esteeming the self, social science actually devises the self and links it to a vision of the social good and a program of reform. In short, social scientists have helped to produce a set of social relationships and causal relations where there were none before.

Social science has been instrumental in generating a self capable of self-governance, but it is a decidedly unscientific enterprise. In the end, social scientists themselves eschew the importance of evidence: "Our purpose is to build a *prima facie* case for the importance of self-esteem in the causation of violent crimes. Public policy does not wait for final proof in other realms. . . . We see no need to be defensive about advocating the importance of self-esteem."[23] The obvious question is why social science is a necessary member of a coalition for building a *prima facie* case for self-esteem. If the case is to be built *prima facie*, why call for more funding to gather evidence in the form of social science research? The answer lies, I think, in the productive capacities of social scientific research. It is social scientific research that produces the subject as one who lacks self-esteem, and it is social science research that sets the terms for telling the truth of that subject. Finally, it falls to social science research to establish policy measures to regulate the subject according to that truth. In a turn of phrase taken from Pierre Bordieu, from professing a faith in self-esteem for its liberatory properties, experts have turned self-esteem into a profession.[24]

Social service providers and researchers will earn high salaries from the self-esteem movement, and new programs are proliferating. "Empowerment" and "self-esteem" are almost mandatory in mission statements and grant applications for nonprofit agencies. But self-esteem advocates are not merely the poverty pimps of the 1990s (although there is certainly plenty of evidence for that characterization).[25] It is a mistake to focus solely on the immediate economic and professional interests of service providers. Program directors and researchers may profit from the advances of the self-esteem movement, but that does not fully explain why or how people come to understand themselves as lacking self-esteem. It is equally partial to characterize self-esteem programs as obscuring or neglecting the "real" underlying causes (e.g., poverty, sexism, racism) of the lack of self-esteem. The self-esteem movement is not conceived on the level of ideology. It is not a ruse, a panacea, a cynical plot; it is a form of governance.

Despite the failure of social scientists to discern any causal relationship between violence and self-esteem, a correlative relationship has worked its way into law. I quote from Assembly Bill No. 3659, which established the California Task Force: "The findings of the Commission on Crime Control and Violence Prevention included scientific evidence of the correlation between violent antisocial behavior and a lack of self-esteem, to wit: 'A lack of self-esteem, negative or criminal self-image and feelings of distrust and personal powerlessness are prevalent among violent offenders and highly recidivistic criminals.'"[26] The Task Force adapted the model of the Commission on Crime Control for its own "citizens' effort" to secure funding for further research and took from the field of criminology its methods of applying and organizing knowledge.

It is significant, of course, that the new technology of self-esteem is produced in part out of methods devised for the prevention of crime and the supervision of prisoners. From analyzing among the causes of the bloody Attica prison riot a decline in the self-esteem of guards who were not consulted before their powers were reduced, reviewers leap immediately to the policy implications of that analysis for relationships between clients and staff, doctors and patients, teachers and students, parents and children.[27] The whole of society and all its designated "social problems" become the location for the deployment of this new technology of subjectivity. A whole society of esteemed, estimated, quantified, and measured individuals can replace a citizenry defined by their lack of self-esteem. It is also important to remember that the language of empowerment and self-esteem emerged out of social movements. Liberation is clearly tied to discipline in the discourses of self-esteem in more ways than I can chronicle here. I mention just two.

First, so-called welfare dependency, alcoholism, and teen pregnancy are pathologized and criminalized alongside violence, child abuse, and illegal drug use. This move is accomplished by relating the "low self-esteem" of welfare recipients, for example, to their failure to act politically, to participate in their own empowerment, to engage in fulfilling the social obligation of "responsible citizenship." According to the California Task Force report, welfare recipients fail to fulfil their responsibilities to society because they lack self-esteem, a deficiency demonstrated by their being on welfare in the first place. Second, the knowledge originally applied to the government, control, and reform of criminals and "antisocial behavior" is now applied throughout the social body: the overt use of technologies of surveillance and control in the field of criminality are displaced by the technology of self-government applied to welfare recipients and alcoholics.

According to the California Task Force, the "social vaccine" must be applied at all levels of society. Family, work, government — all areas of society must be integrated by the principles of self-esteem and personal and social responsibility: "In the twenty-first century every government level in the state and each of its programs are designed to empower people to become self-realizing and self-reliant. . . . Every citizen (and noncitizen as well) recognizes his or her personal responsibility for fully engaging in the political process, and he or she recognizes the possibility for positively affecting every other person in every situation and relationship."[28] The characterization of the future in present tense notwithstanding, the discourse of self-esteem is aimed at constituting a just and democratic society. To get there, rather than revealing our opinions and persuading others to act in concert with us, we should work to achieve self-esteem, which has to do with our reputation with our selves. Constituting a state of esteem has nothing to do with traditionally conceived public life and speech. A state of esteem can be founded upon the inner dialogue between self and self.

From the prison cell to the whole of society, individuals in isolation can act to bring about a social and democratic revolution. Steinem believes that "self-esteem plays as much a part in the destiny of nations as it does in the lives of individuals; that self-hatred leads to the need either to dominate or to be dominated; that citizens who refuse to obey anything but their own conscience can transform their countries; in short, that self-esteem is the basis of any real democracy."[29] Given the possibility of thus aligning political power and self-esteem, what is the answer to Tocqueville's question about the possibility for resistance to the established order in isolation?

A New Science of Politics

Foucault and feminism have shown how individuals come to understand themselves as the subjects of sexuality and gender, respectively. Similarly, I am arguing that individuals learn to recognize themselves as subjects of democratic citizenship and so become self-governing. As with technologies and discourses of sexuality and gender, it is possible to give a history of the fabrication of citizen-subjects and of their relation to the social order. But what Foucault and feminism have not elaborated, Alexis de Tocqueville took as a guiding question: namely, why do these forms of power, citizenship, and subjectivity emerge only with democracy? How does governance become a question of self-governance in a democracy?

The capacities of citizens to govern their selves as well as the conditions of self-government underwent dramatic changes in the nineteenth century (Chapter 2). In America, the difficulties that Tocqueville encountered in distinguishing between despotism and democracy reveal that self-government entails more than the exercise of subjectivity; it entails also the subjection of the self.

Ostensibly, democracy liberated political subjects, transforming them overnight into political citizens. A society in which a citizen is subject to the rule of another is, ipso facto, not a democracy. (Chapter 1 explained the flaws in Tocqueville's citizen/subject contrast.) The democratic citizen who participates directly in government, in self-rule, thereby avoids subjection, according to Tocqueville's first volume of *Democracy in America*. But the line between the subjectivity of citizens and their subjection was not so clear, he discovered; by the time he finished the second volume, he seemed unable to distinguish either democracy from its tendencies toward despotism or the sovereignty of the masses from their subjection.

Both despotism and democracy relied upon isolated and powerless citizens, according to Tocqueville. Under *despotism*, subjects were simply unfree and isolated. In a *democracy*, under conditions of equality, citizens were isolated and made powerless by the freedom granted to each singly; although free, they were relatively powerless as isolated individuals. Hence, the power of numbers became the sine qua non of democratic power and stability. In order to exercise self-government, citizens had to act in concert and combine forces to wield any power and guard against the tendency of democracies toward despotism.

The same democratic conditions — individual equality and individual freedom — made combining numbers very difficult, however. "Since in times of equality no man is obliged to put his powers at the disposal of another, and no one has any claim of right to substantial support from his fellow men, each one is both independent and weak," wrote Tocqueville. "These two conditions, which must be neither seen quite separately nor confused, give the citizen of a democracy extremely contradictory instincts."[30] Getting independent citizens to participate and take an interest in the life and well-being of society was no small task. In a chapter titled "That the Americans Combat the Effects of Individualism by Free Institutions," Tocqueville insisted that local and associational freedoms — political freedoms — were the only safeguards against despotism because they ensured the capacity of citizens to govern themselves by providing the training and the taste for freedom.

Yet the features of either despotism or democracy led citizens to neglect their political freedoms, which, from disuse, were rendered powerless against despotism. "Equality puts men side by side without a link to hold them firm. Despotism raises barriers to keep them apart. It disposes them not to think of their fellows and turns indifference into a sort of public virtue."[31] Tocqueville recognized that although the police and the state could prevent action by means of outright domination and force, they could not produce the active cooperation and participation of citizens. Democratic governance relied upon a productive (rather than a repressive) form of governance, which eluded the grasp of the state.[32] To guide and govern a democracy, Tocqueville called for a "new science of politics."[33] Democratic participation was not clear-cut or naturally occurring; it was something that had to be solicited, encouraged, guided, and directed. Hence, the new science of politics needed to develop technologies of citizenship and participation.

Isolated from one another by their freedom, individuals required an artificially created solidarity: namely, a science of association. "In democratic countries knowledge of how to combine is the mother of all other forms of knowledge; on its progress depends that of all the others."[34] Even the legal recognition of associations, previously considered a dangerous source of disorder, was not enough to ensure democratic order if citizens could not be led to exercise their political freedoms; the capacity of citizens to exercise self-government itself had to become a matter of government.

In short, the threat of despotism and disorder came not from the unruly but from the indifferent, the apathetic.[35] "Individually weak citizens form no clear conception in advance of the power they might gain by combining; to understand that, they must be shown it."[36] Citizens had to be made to act: first, they must know how to get together, to amass themselves to act in concert; second, they must desire to do so. The former could be accomplished through the science of association; the latter was a matter of what Tocqueville called "enlightened self-interest, or "interest rightly understood: "When no firm and lasting ties any longer unite men, it is impossible to obtain the cooperation of any great number of them unless you can persuade every man whose help is required that he serves his private interests by voluntarily uniting his efforts to those of all the others."[37] Persuading citizens to tie their self-interest and their fate voluntarily to society was the key to stability without the use of force.

The republican preoccupation with civic virtue — overcoming one's self-interest to take up the common interest — was replaced, according to Tocqueville, by the discipline that led to actions incited by "enlightened self-interest." Democratic political action was further distinguished by a "general rule" that links citizens to society: "The doctrine of self-interest properly understood does not inspire great sacrifices, but every day it prompts some small ones; by itself it cannot make a man virtuous, but its discipline shapes a lot of orderly, temperate, moderate, careful, and self-controlled citizens. If it does not lead the will directly to virtue, it establishes habits which unconsciously turn it that way."[38]

Tocqueville learned about discipline and enlightened self-interest from his study of prisons. As others have pointed out, he learned that prison discipline could "make up" good citizens even if it could not produce virtuous men.[39] One must not make too much of the prison as a model for democratic government, however.[40] The prison may serve as a perfect model for despotism but not for democracy. The task Tocqueville set himself was to discover those aspects of democracy that could be mobilized against despotism, despite the similarities he saw between the two forms of governance. If the condition of equality generalized the techniques of the prison to voluntary relations, the problem was to turn voluntary power relationships against despotism.

Tocqueville claimed that neither despotism nor democracy had been given shape by institutions and laws. Democracy was a certain kind of society. The tendency toward despotism lay less in the governing institutions of democracy than in the techniques by which democracy was governed. The condition of democratic equality and individual isolation led to the contradictory propensity of democratic citizens, on the one hand, to become ungovernable in their independence and, on the other hand, to submit in powerlessness to any authority powerful enough to command them.

"Nevertheless, I am convinced that anarchy is not the greatest of the ills to be feared in democratic times, but the least. Two tendencies in fact result from equality: the one first leads men directly to independence and could suddenly push them right over into anarchy; the other, by a more round-about and secret but also a certain road, leads them to servitude."[41]

Tocqueville's new science of politics, then, was concerned not with po-litical institutions but with preserving democratic freedom and the power of citizens within the voluntary relations of society. The ties that citizens needed to cultivate were not political but social (associational), even if their object was political; their fabrication marked the dislocation of the politi-cal, the state, and the emergence of "the social" in the nineteenth century alongside the birth of the social sciences. Associations — organized to build bridges, to develop the arts and sciences, to do business — were useful for cementing individual citizens' desires and goals to a vision of what was good for society. With no apparent coercion or centralized state action, voluntary associations could ensure a united citizenry and a stable society.

Democracy entailed the transformation of politics from an activity dependent upon a conception of public (as opposed to private) life to a matter of social life and the life of society. For democracy to meet the requirement of getting individuals to act together in concert as citizens, Tocqueville initially sounded a common republican theme: "As soon as common affairs are treated in common, each man notices that he is not as independent of his fellows as he used to suppose and that to get their help he must often offer his aid to them."[42] In a mass democracy, however, as opposed to a republic, a single public sphere could not extend far enough to impress upon all the citizens their need of one another to maintain sta-bility. Republican self-government was understood to be a part-time activ-ity taking place within the restricted public sphere and concerning matters of public (shared) importance; freedom and politics were located in the re-stricted public sphere. In a democracy, by contrast, democratic freedom and hence the activities of self-government underwent a despatialization and were then located in associations and in the capacities and actions of individuals.

The capacity of citizens to be self-governing in a republic depended upon institutions that disappeared under the conditions of democracy. In a republic, a concern for the common weal was grounded in the fact that public life was restricted to male property owners and soldiers. Tocqueville claimed that the legislators of American democracy knew that a single pub-lic sphere could not extend the awareness of mutual dependence to an isolated citizenry; hence, the whole of society had to be governmentalized and venues constructed for citizens to take care of organizing and governing themselves.

Voluntary associations, while avoiding the politically disabling expansion of government into the activities of citizens, extended the reach of power by getting people to act for themselves. Tocqueville asked, "What political power could ever carry on the vast multitude of lesser undertakings which associations daily enable American citizens to control?"[43] Associations artificially extended the reach of government into ungoverned relations.

Still, what was it that distinguished democracy from despotism? The answer lay not in politics or institutions but in the relationship of the individual to society. Again, Tocqueville was struck by the absence of visible official governmental powers and actions in America.[44] Moreover, he was dumbstruck and terrified by the invisible governance to which citizens were subject: "Thus I think that the type of oppression which threatens democracy is different from anything there has ever been in the world before. . . . I have myself vainly searched for a word which will exactly express the whole of the conception I have formed."[45] What Tocqueville called "despotism," for lack of a better expression, he described as a condition of holding society — its interests, privileges, wisdom, and power — above the individual. Despotism was the threat not of too much government but of not enough. "The idea of intermediary powers is obscured and obliterated. The idea of rights inherent in certain individuals is rapidly disappearing from mens' minds; the idea of the omnipotence and the sole authority of society at large is coming to fill its place."[46] Powers of government, then, were transferred from the government and from the individual onto society at large; society was granted "its duty, as well as its right to take each citizen by the hand and guide him."[47]

We have traditionally understood Tocqueville to be holding out the tyranny of the majority or society writ large as a threat to the subjectivity, actions, and independence of individuals. For him, however, democratic government did not pit the individual citizen *against* collective society, for unlike the state, society had no agency or power of its own to wield. The dangerous tendency in a democracy was not toward tyranny, domination, or forced conformity but toward an invisible and gentle subjection. The tutelary power of associations, which could lead citizens to exercise their subjectivity and to act upon their enlightened self-interest, could also lead them into complete subjection. "Each individual lets them put the collar on, for he sees that it is not a person, or a class of persons, but society itself which holds the end of the chain."[48] Citizens obeyed the call of society at large; self-guided, without chains, without force, they quietly placed themselves in the hands of society and mobilized in society's interest.

Tutelary power could be easily combined with outward forms of political freedom because it was society at large, not a class or a tyrant, placing citizens in chains. Society was that which stood above. The individual citizen was not pitted *against* the majority but was artificially linked *to* the majority by discipline and association. The distinction between despotism and democracy rested on the degree to which tutelary powers acted for individuals rather than guiding them to act for themselves. That is to say, democracy depended upon the social construction of citizens capable of governing themselves. "We should therefore direct our efforts, not against anarchy or despotism, but against the apathy which could engender one or the other almost indifferently."[49] It was upon the small and daily routines of social life that self-government depended. "Subjection in petty affairs is manifest daily and touches all citizens indiscriminately. It never drives men to despair, but continually thwarts them and leads them to give up using their free will."[50]

Recovery of the Will

Tocqueville overestimated the tendency of democracies toward despotism because he underestimated the successes of the social sciences and social reformers at developing technologies of citizenship. For example, he and Gustave de Beaumont found prison reformers in the United States a bit overzealous: "Philanthropy has become for them a kind of profession, and they have caught the *monomanie* of the penitentiary system, which to them seems the remedy for all the evils of society."[51] Today, self-esteem is one example of our reformers' *monomanie*. It is an innovation in the means of governing a democratic society.

The self-esteem movement is but one in a long line of technologies of citizenship and continual efforts to reform the liberal arts of government. Democracy is entirely dependent upon the technologies of citizenship developed in social movements, in public policy research, and in the sciences of human development, and elsewhere. The constitution of the citizen-subject requires technologies of subjectivity, technologies aimed at producing happy, active, and participatory democratic citizens. These technologies rarely emerge from the Congress; more often they emerge from the social sciences, pressure groups, social work discourses, therapeutic social service programs, and so on. Their common goal is to get the citizen to act as his or her own master.

Social reform begins with the acknowledgment that democratic government is limited in its capacity to govern. Democratic government relies upon citizens to subject themselves to power voluntarily. Here is the state of California saying, go ahead and democratize the family, the workplace, the schools: "Sometimes we feel that if we create democracy in the home, work place or school, we will undercut someone's authority and encourage irresponsibility. In fact, democracy works well only when we all exercise self-discipline and personal and social responsibility."[52]

Of course, not everyone can be "vaccinated," and those who lack self-esteem will presumably continue to abuse, haunt, rob, reproduce and otherwise bring ill health upon the social body.[53] Nevertheless, as a cure for so many ills, self-esteem means about as much as "positive thinking" meant in the 1970s, "empowerment" in the 1980s, and "enterprise" in the 1990s. We are not entering the age of an all-powerful therapeutic state, or a state of complete subjection, for we are still citizens. Yet thousands of people now define their lack of power and control in the world as attributable to their lack of self-esteem. Gloria Steinem, spokeswoman for the National Organization for Women (NOW), one of the largest feminist associations, today attributes the failures of her political career and the feminist movement to her own lack of self-esteem.

More important, state government documents such as those from California that I have considered here do not create citizen-subjects by themselves. Nor do the therapists, mothers, and politicians who vaccinate citizens with self-esteem bear the responsibility for creating citizen-subjects. Self-esteem is but one in a long line of technologies that avail the citizen of him- or herself. Self-rule remains essential to democratic stability, and so the relationship of self to self is a political relationship, although one that is more dependent upon voluntarily applied technologies of selfhood than upon coercion, force, or social control engineered from above.

Self-esteem advocates, including Steinem, may not recognize the extent to which personal life is the product of power relations, the extent to which personal life is governed and is itself a terrain of government. The "inner voice" she teaches us to listen to is the voice of pure and unmediated self-knowledge. She assumes that women have a natural subjectivity that is hindered or repressed by power, rather than shaped and constituted by power. Steinem fails to grasp the difficulty of distinguishing subjectivity from subjection.

Self-esteem as a social movement links subjectivity and power in a way that confounds any neat separation of the "empowered" from the powerful. Most important, the self-esteem movement advocates a new form of governance that cannot be critically assessed by separating public from private, political from personal. Too much is left out by critics of the self-esteem movement who continue to think of power and resistance in paired opposition: individual and collective, public and private, political and personal. What these criticisms omit, I contend, is the extent to which the citizen is (like inequality, poverty, and racism) the product of power relations, the outcome of strategies and technologies developed to create everything from autonomy and empowerment to self-esteem. External powers act upon the terrain of the self, but we also act upon ourselves, particularly according to such models of self-help as the self-esteem movement. In the words of Hacking, critics "leave out the inner monologue, what I say to myself. They leave out self-discipline, what I do to myself. Thus they omit the permanent heartland of subjectivity."[54] We might add that they leave out self-government, how we rule ourselves.

Tocqueville attributed to the general "equality of conditions" shared by American citizens their role in generating stability. What has become evident since is that even in a society deeply divided by inequalities of race, class, and gender, political stability is relatively secure and overt resistance rare. Although the absence of open conflict is notable, social science that proposes a lack of something (of resistance, of a social movement, of a consciousness of race, class, or gender, of self-esteem) is a productive science that plays a large role in democratic government.

I have outlined a history of the present "state of esteem," a new political order founded upon the self. Needless to say at this point, self-esteem does not divert the political will of feminism toward personal therapy. Already, self-esteem is being replaced by the new *monomanies* of "enterprise," "community," and antiracism. The history of the self-esteem movement illustrates only that self-governance is still a condition of democracy.

5

Welfare Queens: Ruling by Number

Welfare recipients were obviously intimidated and dominated by state power, excluded from political self-representation and participation. Yet, during the Reagan era in America the so-called welfare queen was also sovereign over the system of welfare. The ultimate con, she outsmarted the system; she was a grifter, a fraud, who "abused" the desire of taxpayers to help the down-and-out. As such, she was both sovereign and subject simultaneously. According to Nietzsche, that subjects can be held accountable is a condition of their appearance. Yet the welfare queen was accountable in a very strange way, I argue: that is, she was the subject of numbers and the innovations in auditing techniques applied to welfare case data in the 1970s.

That the welfare queen was both sovereign and subject makes her a typical liberal democratic citizen-subject in the terms of my argument thus far. But not all liberal democratic citizen-subjects are alike; there is more than one kind, and welfare queens are just one example. To argue that the welfare queen is a citizen-subject is surprising, perhaps, given that her status is so often taken to be an effect of illiberal ideology and racism, not of liberal welfare state practices. Critics sympathetic to the welfare state and welfare activists believe that the "myth" of the black welfare queen is used to legitimate the excessive and punitive practices of the welfare state by mobilizing public prejudice against welfare recipients and black women. For example, Lucie White writes, "'welfare fraud'" has long been one of the dominant themes expressing the ambivalence, indeed aversion, within modern political culture, to welfare. 'Fraud' connotes an idea — a negative image of the 'typical welfare recipient.' At the same time, it justifies an elaborate regime for monitoring eligibility determinations and restricting the welfare rolls."[2] Accounting for the "myth" entails something more than exposing the lies about welfare queens, however.

The election campaign mantra for conservatives in the 1980s, "going after fraud, waste and abuse in the welfare system," meant prosecuting the welfare queen and holding her accountable for "cheating" the system and corrupting the welfare state. Welfare rights advocates argued that welfare recipients were easy targets, the scapegoats of the right-wing backlash that followed upon the gains of the civil rights movement and the growth of entitlement programs throughout the 1970s. The argument of welfare advocates was that poor women could not represent themselves, and so they made easy targets during the fiscal crisis of the 1980s.

In other words, welfare rights advocates argued that the assault upon the welfare queen was due to her powerlessness to represent herself. The conflict was understood to be between the interests of the Reagan administration, which was set on turning back entitlement programs, and those of the welfare recipients who relied upon those programs. For example, Piven and Cloward explain that the Reagan administration scapegoated AFDC recipients because, "unlike elderly or disability claimants, AFDC recipients are unorganized and are therefore unable to respond to charges effectively. . . . singling out AFDC inevitably becomes an attack on minorities."[3] It is the welfare queen's unaccountability, then, her voicelessness, her absence from the stage of politics that accounts for her status as a scapegoat.

That argument is no doubt familiar to most readers. Nevertheless, I argue that Nietzsche was right: the accountability of the subject is a condition of her appearance. It was not the powerlessness of the welfare queen or her subjection that made her available as a scapegoat; rather, it was her sovereignty, her accountability, that was the condition of her appearance. It is the fact that she was represented and constituted as a quantifiable and calculable citizen-subject that accounts for her. I argue that the welfare queen's condition of appearance was established long before Reagan made her guilty for the overgrown welfare state. It was the Carter administration's new auditing techniques and case evaluation standards that became the condition for the appearance of the welfare queen.

In other words, my explanation reverses the ones given by Piven, Cloward, and White: excessive, punitive, and productive welfare practices constitute the myth of the stereotypical welfare queen. The stereotype does not justify or legitimate welfare practices; rather, those practices justify stereotypes.

The reason for my reversal is strategic. I indirectly confirm Nietzsche's claim not for philosophical reasons but for political ones. The welfare rights movement and its strategists have historically sought to combat the racist and ideological representation of the welfare queen by calling upon her to represent herself, to act in her own interests with others of her kind.[4] In other words, critics seek to mobilize the very myth of the welfare queen they seek to debunk. To start from the fact of political exclusion and then argue for the inclusion of poor women's voices in debates over welfare reform, to argue for their self-representation, is already to take the welfare queen for granted, to take her for "real." Indeed, any causal explanation, however critical, that can be drawn between the mythical figure of the black welfare queen and the welfare system mistakenly takes her for "real." So, by staging a reversal of causal terms, I risk also taking a fiction for a fact.

That risk is worth taking — again, for strategic reasons. Another welfare rights strategy is to "speak truth to power," to educate the public on the facts in order to depose the myth of the welfare queen. Later on, I explain further why that strategy is doomed to failure. No matter how many times the facts are marshaled against the myths of welfare, the facts of the matter do not provide a leghold in the politics of representation. To argue that not all welfare recipients are guilty of fraud fails on two fronts. First, AFDC grants were so low in the 1980s that only those with public housing in some states could get by on a welfare budget; therefore, the guilt of any welfare recipient who lived relatively well was presumed by welfare fraud investigators. (This was established for the first time, however, only in 1997.)[5] Second, to defend the innocence of the welfare queen is to undermine the conditions of her appearance. This is a somewhat different but closely related trap to the one I laid out in the introduction to this book.

How do we account for the fact that the welfare queen's existence is a myth? The short answer is, by accounting: it is numbers that constitute the body of the mythical queen. I argue that it is crucial to study the numerical terms of her embodiment — to account for the fact that she is embodied, rather than to account for what is done to her body. That the stereotypical welfare queen is black, lazy, oversexed, and cunning, I argue, does not necessarily point the right course for political resistance. If we were to end our critique with the claim that welfare cheats were excluded from democratic politics, racially stereotyped in the media, and scapegoated by politicians, we would fail to see that the appearance of this mythical queen was premised upon her accountability, not her race, class, gender, or kinship ties.

Judith Butler notes a dual relation of the subject to power in her analysis of gender and feminist politics: "It is not enough to inquire into how women might become more fully represented in language and politics. Feminist critique ought also to understand how the category of 'women,' the subject of feminism, is produced and restrained by the very structures of power through which emancipation is sought."[6] Taking my cue from Butler and Nietzsche, I argue that a critique of welfare cannot simply call for more participation on the part of or in the name of welfare recipients in the definition and provision of their own needs—a struggle Nancy Fraser calls "the politics of need interpretation."[7] (The same might be said of job training now that federal entitlement programs like Aid to Families with Dependent Children have ended.) Before calling upon welfare recipients to act in their own interests and represent themselves politically as recipients, one must, to paraphrase Butler, examine how the category "welfare queen," the subject of welfare, is both produced and restrained by the relations of rule we call "welfare."[8]

To take the welfare queen for "real," to ask her to speak on her own behalf and to act in her own interests, is to foreclose the possibility that she could refute or refuse the terms of welfare. Critical strategies for mobilizing welfare recipients, discussed in Chapter 3 and below, typically seek to mobilize the subject-effects of power rather than mobilize against the relations of rule that produce those effects.

Moreover, critical strategies insist that recipients leave the strategic field of power in which they are constituted (just as Charity Organization Society home visitors displaced poor people) to enter the public sphere of politics. Critics of the liberal welfare state too often take the state itself to be the boundary of the political.

Policing Democracy

A welfare-fraud suspect was a subject of welfare — of eligibility criteria in a means-tested program — rather than a subject of the liberal state, a subject of administrative procedure rather than constitutional due process, a subject of error rates rather than civil rights. She did not break the law, but she received a grant for which she was "ineligible." The welfare administration's techniques of fraud detection — statistics, accounting, data matching, hotlines, calculations of cost and benefit — provided the political rationality which governed poor women's citizenship in terms of "waste, fraud, abuse, and error."[9]

Unlike that of citizens generally, a recipient's *freedom* was not the condition of her subjection; it was her *eligibility* to receive AFDC, which was quantifiable and calculable.[10] Welfare recipients were eligible for welfare not on the basis of being citizens but on the basis of a means test, a calculation of their eligibility. (This is not to say that freedom cannot be quantified or calculated, only less obviously.) Eligibility criteria set the terms of welfare and conferred a unity on welfare recipients so that then, and only then, was it possible to govern them according to those criteria.

That unity, however, was purely the product of numbers. The uniformity of numbers does not represent the realities of poor women's lives or their solidarity. Lucie White describes the life of Mrs. G., an AFDC recipient accused of welfare fraud: "In order to participate in AFDC, Mrs. G had no choice but to conform her life to the conditions the program imposed." Mrs. G. was "compelled to assent" to the rules of welfare.[11] Welfare, like liberal democratic government in general, is both voluntary and coercive.

The "voluntary" subjection of the welfare applicant to administrative rules in return for money, vouchers, and services, made her immediately subject to a whole series of double-binds that circumscribed her choices, not the least of which was trading her constitutional rights for a welfare check. Administrative laws and procedures determined not only her political and public behavior but the terms on which she could discuss and handle the basic and mundane aspects of her everyday life: where she could live and with whom, what she could buy and where, whom she could trust.

First, unlike procedures for dealing with most felonies, the investigation and prosecution of welfare fraud were only rarely carried out in criminal courts or governed by the rules of due process.[12] The presumption of guilt was endemic, and recipients had to prove that they were *not* guilty in administrative hearings. Everyone knew that families could not survive on AFDC grants alone, since they rarely approached 70 percent of the federal poverty level. The first premise of welfare-fraud investigations, therefore, was that anyone living in relative stability must be cheating the system somehow.

Second, investigations usually took place in administrative settings — having moved out from an overcrowded criminal justice system — in which one had no right to legal counsel; neither the rules of evidence nor the final authority were clearly determined; and cases could be turned over to county prosecutors at any time.

Third, anyone and any number of agencies could initiate a fraud investigation in most states. A disgruntled lover, the landlord, a father attempting to evade child support payments, or a postal worker could call a state welfare-fraud hotline anonymously. A computer match from another bureaucracy spit out a notice to attend an eligibility hearing. Child-protection services could threaten an investigation in order to achieve anything from getting a woman to agree to therapy to taking her children away. The suspicion of welfare-fraud was constantly repeated to recipients in standard eligibility meetings and subsequent verification actions. Fraud hotline posters were often conspicuous in waiting rooms.

Finally, investigations could be conducted on the agency, county, city, state, and federal levels — even by private investigators, under county contract, who earned a percentage of the amount recouped in fraud convictions and overpayment designations. Tracing the lines of authority for the systematic harassment of welfare recipients is extremely difficult, because power was exercised in innumerable locations. (Recall my search for an authority behind the Dumpster lockup in the introduction.)

Welfare fraud did not link women in poverty to the state so much as link databases for computer cross-matches between agencies — the IRS, SSI, AFDC, Department of Labor, and even state lotteries — in a vision of "system integrity." Welfare fraud administration was a strategy to clean up, police, account for, and discipline an unruly welfare program, not to discipline recipients. Its policing of numbers and strategies for ferreting out "waste, fraud, abuse, and error," however, had a decisive disciplinary and productive effect on welfare recipients. Welfare recipients were substantiated by eligibility criteria and then, as recipients, their continued eligibility was regulated by the terms of welfare.

Mythical Queens

If eligibility criteria produced welfare recipients as a group, how is it that welfare recipients and especially "welfare cheats" were so often stereotyped as black? How were the terms of welfare inscribed onto the body of "the black welfare queen?" Why was the racist and sexist narrative of the black welfare queen repeated so often? Strangely, not one of the professional and governmental publications on welfare fraud that I have read specifically mentions the racial breakdown of fraud, and not one accounting innovation specifically targeted or counted "welfare cheats" by race.

The allusions and allegations made by Ronald Reagan are legendary for legitimating the allegedly popular stereotypes that equated welfare and race. Proudly illiberal, Reagan charged that welfare was not a solution to the inequality that flowed from capitalism; rather, welfare was the cause of inequality. The narrative he spun on the welfare queen took on the quality first of an explanation for the "welfare mess" and, second, of a clarion call to taxpayers in revolt to clean up that mess. As Wahneema Lubiano notes, Reagan's vituperative narrative made all recipients black and all guilty of fraud. Lubiano points out that the "real" facts of welfare and race matter very little, because the myths narrated by Reagan took on the appearance of reality: "And it does not matter that all such children needing state care are not black, or that poverty and unemployment are reasons that they need state care; what matters, what resonates in the national mind's eye, is the constant media-reinforced picture of the welfare queen — always black."[13]

I argue, following Lubiano, that the black welfare queen is never actually embodied; she is and remains a fiction or, rather, she is embodied as a fiction. There is no "real" woman who matches the stereotype. Lubiano is right that the media representation of the queen was a myth. But where does that leave us strategically? We are still armed only with the facts set against the myth — and as Lubiano demonstrates, in the politics of representation the facts don't matter.

From my perspective, it is crucial to study the terms of her embodiment, not her actual body. The welfare queen is not only an ideological scapegoat and fictive character, a racial formation, but also a strategic one. Her race and gender embodiment is the product of fictional narratives and rhetorical ploys, but the fact that she has a body is an effect of numbers.

Numbers are methods of inscribing the lives of welfare recipients and rendering them actionable. As Nikolas Rose writes, "Numbers do not merely inscribe a pre-existing reality. They constitute it."[14] This is to say that administrative decisions based on numbers are not designed as they are simply because taxpayers and politicians are racist. Rather, accounting practices constitute the very "realities" they supposedly count. Thus, for strategic reasons, because I agree with Lubiano that the strategy of discounting myths with facts is fruitless, I want to present a new narrative account of the mythical queen's origin.

The policies that constituted and embodied the welfare queen predate Reagan's rhetoric. For all his hate-mongering, Reagan was not the source of the myth, nor were the media. Rather than being an explicit attack on poor black women, the terms of welfare were set to attack "waste, fraud, abuse, and error" in the name of "system integrity." The myth of the welfare queen began to govern the lives of welfare recipients directly only after a series of crises were declared to be threatening the welfare state and democratic government. Following the 1960s surge in the numbers of AFDC recipients, in 1972 the Subcommittee on Fiscal Policy of Congress's Joint Economic Committee declared a "crisis in public welfare." The subcommittee called the welfare system "an administrative nightmare" resulting in "confusion, inefficiency, and lawlessness."[15]

The crisis was discovered under the Nixon administration, where the solution of quality control (QC) was devised. Evelyn Brodkin and Michael Lipsky have pointed out the ways in which QC was used as a means to get the numbers under control, especially error rates in eligibility determinations, and indirectly to reduce the numbers of people on welfare.[16] Brodkin reports that at the Office of Management and Budget (OMB), "officials were scrutinizing the HEW (Health, Education and Welfare) budget, searching for ways to get control over the 'uncontrollable' entitlement in lieu of legislative reform. Error rates presented an obvious target. From the budget analysts' viewpoint, caseload error rates represented more than an indicator of inadequate state management practices. They signalled an unnecessary outflow of federal dollars."[17]

Policies to "enhance system integrity" continued under Carter, who linked the cleanup to a second crisis, the "crisis of democracy": "This Administration has declared war on waste and fraud in government programs. . . . We are concerned with more than saving tax dollars, crucial as that is today. We must restore and rebuild the trust that must exist in a democracy between a free people and their government."[18] The "crisis of democracy" was a political crisis, as Carter pointed out, and had only an indirect relation to welfare. Carter went on, "As a known or suspected part of the total federal budget, losses through fraud, abuse and error may be small. But compared to the tax bill of the average American, those losses are huge — and demoralizing."[19] Thus, Carter transformed the political "crisis of democracy" into a crisis of numbers: the numbers of tax dollars lost to waste, fraud, abuse, and error; the rising numbers of AFDC recipients; and the rising number of taxpayers in revolt. To govern a democracy meant to discipline systems rather than people, to govern at a distance provided by certain auditing techniques.

Carter appointees devised a strategy not to punish the welfare cheat but to dispel the myth of rampant cheating which, Carter felt, threatened the "integrity of the program." In fact, under the direction of Joseph Califano, administrative reforms were intended to document the fact that very few recipients were committing welfare fraud, that there was no real crisis. Califano opened a national conference on "fraud, abuse, and error" with these remarks: "We cannot let a relatively few cheats and chiselers rob the truly needy of the help they need. So we intend to discipline these and other programs — while we fight those who would dismantle them."[20] In order to prove the integrity of welfare administration, Califano introduced even more ways to make welfare recipients calculable.

At the end of a ten-year period of QC innovations, new verification requirements for AFDC eligibility could include photo identification, sometimes fingerprints, two proofs of residency, verification of social security numbers for every family member (even infants), birth certificates, proof of school attendance, and so forth. Lipsky sums up the net effect of QC measures as "bureaucratic disentitlement."[21]

Indeed, these strategies of welfare-fraud prevention — strategies that changed the terms of welfare — made Reagan's attack possible, made the welfare cheat "real." The new terms of welfare included random QC checks, pre-eligibility screening for fraud and errors, and a shift in emphasis from criminal to administrative prosecutions for welfare fraud. Rather than undergoing jury trials and jail time for fraud, recipients were more likely required to pay back any "overpayments" they had received from welfare agencies, perhaps with fines attached — without any proof whatsoever that they had intended to commit fraud.[22] In other words, recipients often paid the price for agency errors much as if they were guilty of fraud.[23]

By transforming the political crisis into a crisis of numbers and transferring it from the political to the administrative realm, Brodkin argues, welfare officials succeeded in "depoliticizing" the crisis by steering a question of policy out of Congress and into the hands of accountants and managers.[24] A concentration on numbers rather than on votes, however, does not necessarily indicate a shift away from politics, conflict, or domination. Nikolas Rose relates numbers to democratic politics this way: "Numbers are not just 'used' in politics, they help to configure the respective boundaries of the political and the technical."[25] Rather than "depoliticizing" the exercise of power, then, welfare-fraud strategies give scope and method to the productivity of power.

According to Sheldon Wolin, there is a distinctively political motive for transferring a public and contested issue into the realm of administration and bureaucracy: "In brief, the variability of welfare programs means that at any political moment they can be expanded, sharply modified, reversed, even revoked altogether. Variability is the condition that makes possible two complementary phenomena: a certain kind of flexible power and a certain kind of pliable citizen."[26] This is another way to say that discretion was introduced through the extension of bureaucracy. But even more important, this "flexible power," as Wolin calls it (or bio-power, as Foucault would say), can be mobilized because welfare is rooted in administrative rather than constitutional law, and administrative jurisdictions are discretionary.

Rather than being a "depoliticizing" move, the expansion of administrative domains has served to expand the reach of power, a particularly productive kind of power. Political "justice" and the political crisis of democracy were averted by reforms in which investigators (who could be private investigators under contract to the state; employees of the city, county, state, or federal welfare department; or criminal investigators from the district attorney's office) determine the terms of a "fair" investigation, "fair" evidence, and so on. The political in other words, has fluid rather than fixed boundaries.

Far from being rationalized systems of social domination and control, the methods of welfare-fraud investigation and administration were for policing numbers, not people. Far from being an illiberal strategy or a cynical and conspiratorial effort to disenfranchise certain citizens, welfare-fraud administration was distinctively liberal. The terms of poor women's citizenship were the liberal terms of rights and responsibilities, the terms of a contract between citizen and state.

The Terms of Poor Women's Citizenship

On the back of a typical application for welfare, food stamps, or general assistance, the terms of welfare were listed. Very often, a social worker would ask if the applicant understood these terms and, if so, the welfare worker signed the form as evidence that the applicant has read and understood them. At this time recipients were reminded of the penalties for welfare fraud.[27]

The terms laid out a series of double-binds to which the recipient "consented." They were listed in three parts: rights, responsibilities, and appeals. Rights included, for example, the right to apply for public assistance, the right to privacy, the right to have the application explained to you, and so on.

Responsibilities included informing the case worker of any changes in the data provided on the form: "If you give facts that are not true, or do not report a change, you may be charged with fraud. Any facts that you give may be checked by the county office. Facts that deal with your case can be gotten from other sources only if you agree in writing. However, if you do not give your written consent for us to check with other sources or provide us with other proof of your facts, your application may be denied or your grant stopped."[28] In short, if you chose to exercise your right to privacy, you forfeited your right to assistance.

The agencies that exchanged information included the United States Social Security Administration, Internal Revenue Service, Department of Jobs and Training, Child Support Enforcement, unemployment agencies, AFDC, Medical Assistance, Department of Agriculture, mental health centers, state hospitals and nursing homes, insurance companies, the Department of Public Safety, collection agencies, anyone under contract to the state's Department of Human Services, and social service agencies.[29] Reasons given for obtaining information included the need to decide "if you or your family needs protective services." In other words, for instance, the information could be used against you in a juvenile court if a case was initiated by child-protection services. Information was gathered to be used in a punitive system of "protection."

After this double-bind came a more serious one which claimed that Quality Control might choose a case randomly to verify a recipient's facts against those obtained from third parties. "Even if you do not want the contact made, and you do not give your written consent, the reviewer may still make the contact after telling you." Cooperation was thus compulsory.

This section did several things. First, it clarified that even a county official was not the final arbiter of one's eligibility. Final determination of eligibility was always deferred, never settled, and usually discretionary. No one was in charge here; there was no ultimate authority in rules or in the adjudication of the rules.[30] Second, it established that quality control and welfare-fraud investigation were the same thing. Errors could be caused by either clients or workers, but the recipient paid in either case. The terror of random sampling was duplicated by toll-free welfare-fraud hotlines; anyone could report suspicions about a recipient and some states guaranteed an investigation. The most common callers were postal workers, disgruntled lovers, and ex-husbands. Third, one's consent was absolutely meaningless but absolutely necessary. To be eligible for AFDC one had to comply with the verification process and consent to the invasion of privacy — the assumption of guilt before the law — and anyone who did not consent could be investigated anyway.

The appeals process, if a recipient objected to any of the foregoing terms or the determinations of eligibility based on them, was extremely risky to pursue. Most significantly for anyone who lost an appeal, "any overpayment you get between the effective date of the action and the appeal decision must be refunded to the county office." The appeals process, of course, did not establish precedents for future decisions.[31] Even if one woman appealed and won, the terms of welfare would not change.

As an incentive to states and counties to pursue welfare-fraud investigations and audits, the federal government fined states for error rates that were too high. In my own experience, fraud investigators were sometimes the heroes of local media spots, but in state legislatures and Human Service departments they were routinely despised. The occasional plea sent out to welfare recipients to turn in their own kind in order to legitimate the unpopular AFDC program — an attempt to enlist the participation of recipients further in their own subjection — to my knowledge never recruited great numbers. With no clear lines of authority, how is it possible to account for an exercise of power that had such pervasive effects upon women's citizenship? With so many lines of possible action, how is it possible to understand, let alone resist, the actions that are taken?

The Terms of Resistance

The rules of welfare created a strategic field, a space of calculation, a set of possible actions, and then exploited those possibilities. By "strategic field" I mean a field of possible actions distinct from the centralized authority of the state and the law. It is established by relations of rule that are not specific either to a sphere (public/private) or to a geography (local, state, or federal government), nor is it founded in law. A strategic field is not spatially defined but marked by a variable set of strategies; it is established not only by eligibility requirements but also by various disciplinary measures: quality control procedures, computer data cross-matching, accounting practices, and a model of operation whose consequences are not covered by the law.

Welfare-fraud administration was a method for "acting at a distance" upon welfare recipients.[32] Welfare eligibility rules marked off a strategic field in which setting the goal to clean up data sets, for example, or to catch welfare cheats, utilized strategies that were based on numbers. It was established to discipline not people, per se, but the system of welfare. Nevertheless, numbers were methods of inscribing the lives of welfare recipients and rendering them actionable, as well as fictional. No "real" woman but only an abstract woman, a "case," can be constituted by numbers. The quantification of the lives of certain citizens does not necessarily determine or control their behavior, but it does determine that what is counted will add up to something actionable.

Rather than "depoliticizing" the exercise of power, the strategic field of welfare-fraud accounting gave scope to the productivity of power and linked it to expertise, rules, and criteria for evaluation. I do not want to suggest that the terms of welfare were uttered in a unified or centralized voice. Rather, the fields for running numbers overlapped and intersected with other strategic fields, as when a probation officer, doctor, landlord, or drug counselor shared information with a fraud investigator.

The tactics of one Canadian anti-fraud campaign documented by Jim Torczyner are identical to those common in the United States: "There were no public hearings before the campaign was launched because the investigations were introduced as administrative changes that required no change in law or regulation. Consequently, the parliamentary process was bypassed. Although investigators had no legal authority, they had sweeping discretionary power."[33] The strategic field of power gives broad scope for tracking and accounting for numbers.

As a result, poor women's citizenship in the welfare state was determined not by the law applied to a particular territory but by the terms of welfare or the relations of rule that made up a strategic field. Within the strategic field of welfare fraud the option for recipients to resist were never fully foreclosed, but the relations of rule that constituted the strategic field were multiple, shifting, and often contradictory and insidious. The worst double-bind followed from the fact that AFDC grants were made at levels well below the established poverty line. Everyone knew that welfare grants were not enough to live on and this fact more than any other created an atmosphere of fear and suspicion. Welfare recipients knew, probation officers knew, therapists and ex-boyfriends knew, fraud investigators knew: if you lived in one place and had well-fed and well-cared-for children, you were in all likelihood committing welfare fraud; if you were homeless or living in substandard housing, if your kids were poorly dressed and truant, then you were a likely candidate for child-protection services. In either case, you fell within the jurisdiction of a social service or administrative official.

The test of the strategic value of this account of welfare lies in the new forms of resistance that then can be imagined within that field. I have more to say here about what not to do than about what to do because I am not myself standing in that strategic field. Theory will not solve strategical questions of resistance — those will be solved politically — but political theory does serve the negative task of providing the critical space for unlearning and dehabituating ourselves to accustomed ways of conceptualizing politics.

Critical studies of administrative reform and practice are laced with one central and foundational argument — that bureaucracy and administrative practices function chiefly to "depoliticize" power relationships. According to this logic, when issues leave the arena of the state, they no longer produce conflict because the exercise of power is masked; issues disappear, as it were, from the public consciousness and public debate. I have argued, to the contrary, that the "regulation," "professionalization," or "depoliticization" of social life is better understood as an expansion of the political and an extension of power's reach.

In the field of welfare administration I have shown that transforming political problems into problems of numbers does not so much "depoliticize" an issue as make political and governmental action on that issue possible. Government by numbers, then, indicates an extension of the reach of power rather than its concealment. It all depends on where you look. If you look for a face (a racist politician, a power-hungry social worker), you will be disappointed, because in the strategic field of welfare everyone is accountable but there are no bodies.

Critical theories of "depoliticization" are limited in their potential to imagine new forms of resistance because they fail to account for political power beyond the state.[34] Rather than relocating the analysis of politics itself, critical theorists equate politicization with relocating issues in the public sphere or "the political" by removing them from the "depoliticized" arenas of family, economy, or bureaucracy. By failing to locate possible resistance in the strategic field in which it operates, I argue, critical and democratic theorists too often overlook important possibilities for democratic action and resistance.

Nancy Fraser, whose work exemplifies politically engaged and critical theory of the welfare state, lists four kinds of "client resistance."[35] The first is individual resistance aimed, for example, at extending the administrative jurisdiction of an agency to include the needs of the client; the second, the establishment of informal organizations such as domestic kin networks (documented by Carol Stack)[36] and "survival networks"; and the third, the insistence of clients on the primacy of their own subjective narratives over the therapeutic narratives asserted by the experts. None of these forms of resistance is considered to be "political," however; Fraser reserves the designation "political" for a very specific fourth form of resistance, that of organizing *as welfare recipients*:

> In addition to informal, ad hoc, strategic, and/or cultural forms of resistance, there are also more formally organized, explicitly political, organized kinds. Clients of social welfare programs may join together *as clients* to challenge administrative interpretations of their needs. They may take hold of the passive, normalized, individualized or familialized identities fashioned for them in expert discourses and transform them into a basis for collective political action.[37]

Fraser fixes "political" resistance at the level of identity, a level that then aims resistance at the state.[38] In her account, it is only when we embody the terms of welfare that we are acting "politically." Her account rules out much of what I take to be crucial and possible forms of resistance in the welfare rights movement.

Actions and debates that attempt to resist the fixing of a woman's identity "as a recipient" are not, in Fraser's formulation, explicitly political. This excludes what in my own experience is the most common political practice in welfare rights organizations: debating who counts as a "recipient." In Women, Work and Welfare, a membership organization in Minneapolis, some of the most reliable contests and controversial debates involved setting out terms of resistance. Arguments constantly erupted over who, exactly, should be resisting welfare. Who was and was not a legitimate spokeswoman for recipients? For example, are they/we clients, recipients, participants, welfare moms, queens, single moms, poor moms, members of a gender, a class, a race? How should someone be categorized who is not a recipient but participates in welfare rights struggles? How long should a woman have been on welfare to count as a recipient or spokesperson, or how many years can lapse afterward before she is no longer eligible to fill a board position reserved for "recipients"? What are the terms of resistance that can accommodate all the ways women situate themselves in terms of race and class? Should those who resist do so also in the name of their racial and ethnic affiliations, or only as clients or mothers? These questions and more were persistent and hotly debated in organizational meetings, at social functions, and during demonstrations — everywhere welfare rights activists found themselves.

Establishing the terms and subjects of resistance was an ongoing struggle, part of the everyday politics of resistance. In Fraser's account, an expressly political identity is organized by its location in the welfare state — the waiting room: "Notwithstanding the atomizing and depoliticizing dimensions of AFDC administration, these women were brought together in welfare waiting rooms. It was as a result of their participation as clients, then, that they came to articulate common grievances and act together. Thus the same welfare practices that gave rise to these grievances created the enabling conditions for collective organizing to combat them."[39] In this formulation, borrowed by Fraser from Frances Fox Piven, the explicitly political subjectivity of welfare recipients is rendered merely an organizational and ontological *effect* of the organization of state power, a frozen embodiment of power. To achieve an expressly "political" identity, Fraser and Piven insist, political subjects' identities must cohere through group solidarity, which is bounded by shared interests and a shared location vis-à-vis the state. The waiting room of a welfare office coheres group identity, which can *then* act politically. Politics for these critical theorists is something that follows from the exercise of state power, and resistance results *from* the process by which subjectivities are fixed.

By pointing out the limitations of aligning the terms of resistance with the terms of welfare, I seek to expand democratic debate to encompass the constitutive terms of welfare. Critical accounts of welfare are limited in rendering political identity only in terms of state power and not in terms of politics. Questions of strategy and forms of political resistance always devolve, in Fraser's account (as well as those of the democratic theorists addressed in Chapter 2), back to the state. Although Fraser situates discursive contests over needs "between the political, the economic, and the domestic," and she recognizes the multiple locations or directions from which needs discourses flow and collide, the principal function of "enclaves" (similar to what I have called strategic fields) is to "depoliticize" needs discourses.[40] In order to become "political," then, needs must be brought out of the "enclaves" and "go public." But where, exactly, is "the public?"

Although Fraser brilliantly articulates the creation of new publics and new institutions by feminist activists — exemplified by the movement to assist battered women, she presents the process of politicization as resulting in either the political (politicized) or the administrative (depoliticized) satisfaction of needs. For Fraser, these are not merely multiple sites of power but sites shaped by the primacy and unity of political power in the realm of the state and in the terms of discourse. In my account, however, these borders are not traversed by "runaway needs" and needs discourses so much as they are traversed and linked by strategies and relations of rule. Thus, welfare-fraud investigations link the caseworker, the IRS, child protection, the landlord, the hospital, the family, the social worker, and so on. Traversing this map in the process of "politicizing" needs does not require one to break out of the family, the social, the market, the agency, or the accounting firm but demands that one recognize and resist the political strategies that run across those spheres. Whereas Fraser separates subjectivity from subjection in order to imagine political resistance, I have argued that feminist and democratic critiques of welfare should call into question any form of resistance or critique that separates those terms. Practices of governing and ruling are not restricted to "the political" or to one sphere, and so we must focus on *how* we are governed and by what practices, rather than by which people in which sphere.

What we take for "real" political issues has bound us to forms of resistance that are not effective. For example, Piven and Cloward insist that there are "real" political issues, and then there are those that serve the ideological function of making those "real" issues disappear.

> There are, in other words, problems in the welfare programs. But no serious investigation of "fraud and abuse" would begin with unemployment, food, and welfare programs. It might begin with defense contracts or the tax system, where fraud and profiteering are normal rather than merely rampant, and where the gains made are huge. And one might go to the private vendors associated with the Medicare, Medicaid, and housing programs. For the Reagan administration, however, fraud and abuse are *not the real issues*, and the budget cuts are not directed against these problems. They are directed against the recipients of welfare state benefits.[41]

Welfare rights activists have understood the "welfare queen" to be an ideological ruse to cover up the "real" abuses of power at higher levels of government. The counterattack by welfare rights organizations and advocates aims to expose the faces of "real" fraud, to unmask the irrationality of political leaders for whom welfare-bashing is a political meal ticket. This strategy goes back as far as the struggles of the National Welfare Rights Union led by George Wiley in the 1960s and 1970s, which were aimed at unmasking the "real" welfare crisis and the "real" fraud.[42] But despite the facts, despite the "real," and no matter how many people know about it, making an issue "public" or "politicizing" it is not an effective mode of resistance.

One cannot, of course, simply refuse the terms of welfare, for they are a condition of receiving housing, food, and income.[43] Once one is already defined by the terms of welfare, a different kind of strategy is necessary, a strategy that targets those very terms. Resistance must take the form of a refusal to act *as* a recipient, a refusal to be what our relations to the state have made us. As Foucault suggested, "Maybe the target nowadays is not to discover what we are, but to refuse what we are. We have to imagine and to build up what we could be to get rid of this kind of political 'double bind,' which is the simultaneous individualization and totalization of modern power structures."[44] To hold the productive aspects of power and the liberal arts of government politically accountable, we must imagine a way of politically managing the fact that there is such a thing as the social construction of citizenship — that like welfare queens, all citizens are also subjects.

Conclusion
Iteration

The repetition that citizens are apathetic, too uninterested or too self-interested to engage in politics, is both excited and monotonous, to use a Tocquevilleian phrase. This book has asked what makes that repetition so inexhaustible, so ready at the tip of the tongue. The condition of its utterability is the will to empower. When we hear that subjects are apathetic or powerless and that citizenship is the cure, we are hearing the echo of the will to empower. It is the echo of a way of thinking about politics, power, and democracy that is forever blinded by what is not there.

Even as I write, political scientists are, like Colonel Waring, developing a new cottage industry and new sources of political capital out of waste. Lamenting the loss of "social capital," Robert Putnam asserts that trust, civility, and "civic engagement" are on the wane in America.[1] Americans don't join up as they used to in civic associations, bowling leagues, bridge clubs; we even avoid the neighborhood street-corner chats. We are more likely to write a check than to take part in a rally or listen to a speech. By "social capital," Putnam means "features of social life — networks, norms, trust — that enable participants to act together more effectively to pursue shared objectives."[2] Just when the government is devolving the administration of welfare to the state and local levels, we no longer have the "social capital" necessary to run it. The culprit? According to Putnam, it is television. TV is antisocial. We spend too much time watching rather than associating; our children are socialized and educated via their interaction with TV. "Social capital" is in crisis because we do not get up off the couch and participate civically. The repetitions of the will to empower seem endless.

Like any discourse, the discourses of empowerment are learned, habitual, and material, as Samuel Delaney says.[3] It is quite natural to seek the cause of political problems in order to prescribe a cure. It is my hope that readers of this book will find it harder to pin a political problem on the lack of citizenship. I hope that in its stead we will interrogate what is there in the will to empower, the technologies of citizenship and arts of government by which the various kinds of citizens we have are constituted.

Rather than too few citizens or too little attention to citizenship, we have different kinds of citizens who are recognized not for what they do or what they have been made into but for what they lack. I have argued that the will to empower is a strategy of government, one that seeks solutions to political problems in the governmentalization of the everyday lives of citizen-subjects. Also, I have argued that apathy and powerlessness cannot stand as both the cause and the effect of political problems. For democratic government to work, citizens must be made — which says to me that citizens can be remade, and that the social construction of citizenship is both a promise and a constraint upon the will to empower.

There is more than one kind of citizen-subject. To be clear, I do not argue that there is no difference between citizens and subjects; rather, their differences are a measure of how variously citizens are made. When I say that the citizen is the condition of possibility for democratic politics, I mean not that the citizen is the foundation of democracy but that the making of citizens is a permanent political project for democracy. Is it possible to make new kinds of citizens? Yes. I have argued that they are made all the time. But if their social constitution is erected upon what they are said to lack, then citizens will always fall short of democratic expectations.

This book asks the reader to consider the political effects of the will to empower. Those effects are twofold. First, citizen-subjects are socially constituted, and that means that citizens embody power relations; power is a property of the citizen, and so citizens are always subject in some sense, even if it is to their own self-government. Political power is exercised both upon and through the citizen-subject at the level of small things, in the material, learned, and habitual ways we embody citizenship. At every turn, I find that power in technologies of citizenship and the liberal arts of government. That means that not all powers can be held accountable because they cannot be confronted face to face. We need a different criterion by which to measure democracy, one different from the accountability of power. That power has no face does not mean that it is monstrous, only that it could be.

The second political effect of the will to empower is on the ways that the political is constituted. I have argued that democratic politics is not out there, in the public sphere or in a realm, but in here, at the very soul of subjectivity. Politics is also down there, in the strategic field of small things. For democratic theory to insist upon the autonomy of the political or civil society is, once again, to be blinded by what is not there.

So many of the words I have written here are critical of democratic theory and democratic modes of government that I fear this book will be read as antidemocratic. It is not my intention to deliver a polemic against democracy or against efforts to think it otherwise. What I value most about democracy is that its effects are contingent rather than permanent; it is a strategic field that is never closed to new interventions. The interventions of this book are not intended to vanquish democracy, only to carve out a place in that strategic field for the insights of poststructuralism.

I am not alone in taking a kind of radical democratic solace in the works of Michel Foucault, despite the fact that his work is often taken to betray the promise of democracy. It is widely suspected that Foucault's theory and its application provide us with neither a mode of acting politically within modernity nor a model of the agent who can reconstitute power in a more just and equitable manner. But poststructuralist analyses of power and subjectivity do not merely tear at the foundations of modern democratic theory and citizenship. As I have argued throughout this book, in order to understand how it might be possible to produce citizens otherwise or more democratically, it is necessary to inquire into the constitution of the citizen capable of fashioning a self that is governable.

More implicitly, my argument is pointed to those who will to empower: activists, organizers, educators, social service professionals, and social scientists. That is to say that the argument here is one which, over the years, I have had with myself. This book holds the will to empower to the fire not to destroy it or discount it but to bring both its promise and its dangers to light.

Notes

INTRODUCTION: SMALL THINGS

1. Michel Foucault, "On the Genealogy of Ethics: An Overview of Work in Progress," in *The Foucault Reader*, ed. Paul Rabinow (New York: Pantheon, 1984), 343. The full quotation: "My point is not that everything is bad, but that everything is dangerous, which is not exactly the same as bad. If everything is dangerous, then we always have something to do. So my position leads not to apathy but to a hyper- and pessimistic activism."

2. Many of the insights here are indebted to several recent studies of the political: Judith Butler, "Contingent Foundations: Feminism and the Question of 'Postmodernism,'" in *Feminists Theorize the Political*, ed. Judith Butler and Joan Scott (New York: Routledge, 1992), 3–21; William Connolly, *Political Theory and Modernity* (Madison: University of Wisconsin Press, 1988), and *The Ethos of Pluralization* (Minneapolis: University of Minnesota Press, 1995), esp. the chapter "Democracy and Territoriality"; Ernesto Laclau and Chantal Mouffe, *Hegemony and Socialist Strategy: Towards a Radical Democratic Politics* (London: Verso, 1985); and Nikolas Rose and Peter Miller, "Political Power beyond the State: Problematics of Government," *British Journal of Sociology* 43 (June 1992): 173–205.

3. Butler, "Contingent Foundations," 13.

4. Laclau and Mouffe, *Hegemony*, 181.

5. Gilles Deleuze, "The Rise of the Social," trans. Robert Hurley, foreword to Jacques Donzelot, *The Policing of Families* (New York: Pantheon, 1979), x. In addition to Donzelot's book, I have drawn from others that document the emergence of various social techniques, esp. the essays in Graham Burchell, Colin Gordon, and Peter Miller, eds., *The Foucault Effect: Studies in Governmentality* (Chicago: University of Chicago Press, 1991), and works by Jonathan Crary, Ian Hacking, Mary Poovey, Denise Riley, and John Tagg, some of which are cited elsewhere.

6. J. A. Hobson, *The Social Problem* (1901; Bristol, Eng.: Thoemmes Press, 1996), vi.

7. Mary Poovey, *Making a Social Body: British Cultural Formation, 1830–1864* (Chicago: University of Chicago Press, 1995), 8.

8. Hobson, *Social Problem*, 6.

9. Ibid., vi.

10. Ibid., 4.

11. Ibid., vi.

12. Ibid., 1.

13. Ibid., 7, quoting D. G. Ritchie.

14. Colonel Waring quoted in Martin V. Melosi, *Garbage in the Cities: Refuse, Reform, and the Environment, 1880–1980* (Chicago: Dorsey Press, 1981), 74 (my emphasis).

15. Ibid.

16. Ibid., 29.

17. Quoted in ibid., 79, from "The Sanitary Engineer—A New Social Profession," *Charity and the Commons* (Survey):16 (1906).

18. Melosi, *Garbage*, 72.

19. Lars Eighner, *Travels with Lisbeth: Three Years on the Road and in the Streets* (New York: St. Martin's, 1993), 117.

20. Eighner reports that when a pizza parlor's employees saw him scavenging, they began to hold their garbage inside overnight (ibid., 115).

21. The *Chicago Sun Times*, June 2, 1997, reported that the Drug Enforcement Agency prescribes proper disposal of controlled substances and does prosecute according to the Comprehensive Drug Abuse Prevention and Control Act.

22. "Rural Residents Get Dumpsters Back," *Lewiston Morning Tribune*, (Idaho) March 10, 1993. A newspaper story on the dangers of Dumpster-diving quoted Tom Jackson, president of the Ohio Grocers Association, that if it continued, "the food industry will explore ways to keep divers out of Dumpsters" ("Food Industry, Others Raise Safety Concerns," *Columbus Dispatch*, February 27, 1994).

23. For a brilliant and scathing account of Second Harvest, "a national cartel," a nonprofit whose purpose is to distribute donated food from major corporations to food shelves and soup kitchens, see Theresa Funiciello, *The Tyranny of Kindness: Dismantling the Welfare System to End Poverty in America* (New York: Atlantic Monthly Press, 1993), 123–61. Funiciello argues that Second Harvest's $14 million annual operating budget distributes donations that are largely garbage. It is estimated that up to 60 percent of donations must be thrown out, while corporations pass off the cost of garbage disposal onto food shelves and write off the estimated value of all donations on their taxes, as well as powder their public image. If the $404 million donations in cash and in kind that keep Second Harvest running were simply given to poor people, Funiciello reasons, there would be no hunger in the United States and no cost to taxpayers. As it is, taxpayers subsidize the operation of Second Harvest and private corporations. While Charles Murray and Funiciello both argue for the dismantling of the welfare system because it "makes" the poor, they clearly do so for very different reasons, as I demonstrate in Chapter 1.

24. *Columbus Dispatch*, February 27, 1994.

25. Michael Moore, *Roger and Me* (Burbank, Calif.: Warner Home Video, 1990).

26. League of Women Voters, *The Garbage Primer* (New York: Lyons & Burford, 1993).

27. Albert O. Hirschmann calls this volley *The Rhetoric of Reaction: Perversity, Futility, Jeopardy* (Cambridge, Mass.: Belknap Press of Harvard University Press, 1991).

28. William Connolly, *The Terms of Political Discourse* (Princeton, N.J.: Princeton University Press, 1983).

CHAPTER I. DEMOCRATIC SUBJECTS

1. Tocqueville conceived of power as it was attached to local institutions, not to individuals. See Thomas Dumm, "Freedom and Space," in *Michel Foucault and the Politics of Freedom* (Thousand Oaks, Calif.: Sage, 1996).

2. Ludwig Wittgenstein, *Philosophical Investigations*, 3d ed. (New York: Macmillan, 1968). For an account of the significance of Wittgenstein's language philosophy for political inquiry, see Hanna Fenichel Pitkin, *Wittgenstein and Justice: On the Significance of Ludwig Wittgenstein for Social and Political Thought* (Berkeley: University of California Press, 1972).

3. Judith Butler, *The Psychic Life of Power: Theories in Subjection* (Stanford: Stanford University Press, 1997), esp. 12–18. Butler takes a more critical approach to theories of the subject and subjection and emphasizes that the subject is never simply made but always in the permanent state of becoming.

4. Michel Foucault, "The Subject and Power," in *Michel Foucault: Beyond Structuralism and Hermeneutics*, 2d ed., ed. Herbert L. Dreyfus and Paul Rabinow (Chicago: University of Chicago Press, 1983), 212.

5. The liberal theorist Isaiah Berlin uses "subject" in this sense in his discussion of positive freedom: "I wish to be an instrument of my own, not of other men's acts of will. I wish to be a subject, not an object; to be moved by reasons, by conscious purposes, which are my own." ("Two Concepts of Liberty," in *Four Essays on Liberty* [Oxford: Oxford University Press, 1969], 131.)

6. Eve Sedgewick, *Epistemology of the Closet* (Berkeley: University of California Press, 1990), 11.

7. Samuel Delany gives the clearest possible explanation of how discourse works to shape perception; he argues that discourse is learned, habitual, and material. See his "The Rhetoric of Sex and the Discourse of Desire," in *Heterotopia: Postmodern Utopia and the Body Politic*, ed. Tobin Siebers (Ann Arbor: University of Michigan Press, 1994), 229–72.

8. See, e.g., Jonathan Ned Katz, *The Invention of Heterosexuality* (New York: Plume/Penguin, 1995).

9. I am making an argument analogous to the distinction between sex and gender in feminist theory. If we ask what the difference is between men and women, we presuppose in advance of any analysis that there are men and there are women. To avoid reproducing what Suzanne Kessler and Wendy McKenna call the "incorrigible proposition" that there are two and only two genders, analysis must proceed at the level of their constitution; see their *Gender: An Ethnomethodological Approach* (Chicago: University of Chicago Press, 1978).

10. See William Connolly, *The Ethos of Pluralization* (Minneapolis: University of Minnesota Press, 1995), esp. chap. 3, "Democracy, Equality, Normality."

11. Delany, in "Rhetoric of Sex" (269), calls such discourses "homogenizing discourses."

12. Sheldon Wolin, "What Revolutionary Action Means Today," rpt. in *Dimensions of Radical Democracy: Pluralism, Citizenship, Community*, ed. Chantal Mouffe (London: Verso, 1992), 241.

13. Other strains of radical democracy include workplace democracy and class-based participation, self-development strategies drawing upon Rousseau and the British idealists. See Carole Pateman, *Participation and Democratic Theory* (Cambridge: Cambridge University Press, 1970); Peter Bachrach and Aryeh Botwinick, *Power and Empowerment: A Radical Theory of Participatory Democracy* (Philadelphia: Temple University Press, 1992); C. B. Macpherson, *Democratic Theory* (Oxford: Clarendon, 1973).

14. To name a few (chronologically): Ernesto Laclau and Chantal Mouffe, *Hegemony and Socialist Strategy: Towards a Radical Democratic Politics* (London: Verso, 1985); Iris Marion Young, *Justice and the Politics of Difference* (Princeton: Princeton University Press, 1992); Chantal Mouffe, ed., *Dimensions of Radical Democracy: Pluralism, Citizenship, Community* (London: Verso, 1992); Connolly, *Ethos of Pluralization*.

15. Wolin, "Revolutionary Action," 244.

16. On the centrality of the 1960s to visions of radical democracy, see Meta Mendel-Reyes, *Reclaiming Democracy: The Sixties in Politics and Memory* (New York: Routledge, 1995).

17. Wolin, "Revolutionary Action," 245.

18. Wolin embraces cynicism as a positive sign of a prepolitical rebellion but not itself "genuinely political" (Ibid., 252).

19. Judith Butler points out that "agency belongs to a way of thinking about persons as instrumental actors who confront an external political field. But if we agree that politics and power exist already at the level at which the subject and its agency are articulated and made possible, then agency can be presumed only at the cost of refusing to inquire into its construction." See her "Contingent Foundations: Feminism and the Question of 'Postmodernism,'" in *Feminists Theorize the Political*, ed. Judith Butler and Joan Scott (New York: Routledge, 1992), 13.

For Wolin, instrumental forms of political action are not properly political and may be antidemocratic. "A democratic conception of citizenship, if it means anything at all, means that the citizen is supposed to exercise his rights to advance or protect the kind of polity that depends on his being involved in its common concerns" ("Revolutionary Action," 242).

20. Wolin, "Revolutionary Action," 252.

21. Ibid.

22. Sheldon Wolin, *The Presence of the Past: Essays on the State and the Constitution* (Baltimore: Johns Hopkins University Press, 1989), 150.

23. Ibid., 190–91.

24. See Carole Pateman, "Sublimation and Reification: Locke, Wolin, and the Liberal Democratic Conception of the Political," *Politics and Society* 5 (1975): 441–67. Wolin revises his own view somewhat in "Hannah Arendt: Democracy and the Political," *Salmagundi* 60 (Spring–Summer 1983): 3–19.

25. Wolin, *The Presence of the Past*, 191.

26. Lest I be misread as trashing Wolin's democratic theory, I must add that his "Democracy and the Welfare State: The Political and Theoretical Connections between *Staatsrason* and *Wohlfahrtsstaatsrason*" (in ibid.) largely inspired my own inquiries into the forms of government characteristic of the welfare state. My debt to his work will be evident to anyone familiar with that essay.

27. Wolin, Ibid., 247.

28. Ibid., 247–48. On Arendt's conceptions of the social and the political, see below.

29. For an overview of the debates over power and democracy and an account of "the present impasse," see David Ricci, *Community Power and Democratic Theory: The Logic of Political Analysis* (New York: Random House, 1971).

30. Robert Dahl, *Who Governs? Democracy and Power in an American City* (New Haven: Yale University Press, 1961), 279. Dahl changed his position with the publication of *A Preface to Economic Democracy* (Berkeley: University of California Press, 1985).

31. Dahl, *Who Governs?*, 223–28.

32. See *Report of the National Advisory Commission in Civil Disorders* (New York: Dutton, 1968), esp. the chart on New Haven (n.p.).

33. Frances Fox Piven and Richard A. Cloward, *Regulating the Poor: The Functions of Public Welfare* (New York: Pantheon Books, 1971), 7.

34. A very interesting debate between Linda Gordon and Piven and Cloward appears in *Social Research* 55 (Winter 1988): 609–47. Whereas Piven and Cloward's social control thesis represented the position of the left on welfare for several decades, Gordon's criticism of their thesis exemplifies the subsequent shift on the left, from attacking welfare to defending it against cuts and reforms.

35. Frances Fox Piven and Richard A. Cloward, *Poor People's Movements: Why They Succeed and How They Fail* (New York: Vintage, 1979), 3.

36. Karl Marx, "On the Jewish Question," in *The Marx-Engels Reader*, 2d ed., ed. R. C. Tucker (New York: Norton, 1978).

37. Steven Lukes, *Power: A Radical View* (London: Macmillan, 1974), 27.

38. For a thorough overview of the debates over power, see Peter Bachrach, *The Theory of Democratic Elitism: A Critique* (London: University of London Press, 1969). A short list of substantive studies includes Peter Bachrach and Morton S. Baratz, *Power and Poverty: Theory and Practice* (New York: Oxford University Press, 1970); John Gaventa, *Power and Powerlessness: Quiescence and Rebellion in an Appalacian Valley* (Urbana: University of Illinois Press, 1980).

39. Lukes believed this to be true only in the radical conception of power (see *Power*, 32–33). I am arguing that it is true of the three "faces" of power in general.

40. Ibid., 34.

41. It is important to note that many theorists of participatory democracy hoped that their studies would spark rebellion—Lukes was most explicit on this point—but few hoped their studies would spark revolution, and they carefully distinguished their own class analyses from those of socialists. Peter Bachrach, e.g., wrote in "Class Struggle and Democracy," *Democracy* 2 (Fall 1982): 34, that "militancy and radicalism have been nurtured within the existing hegemonic order. Consequently, the mistake of trying to

inculcate 'socialist consciousness' within the working class must not be repeated while the idea of democracy can still be made to live. Within the context of American experience, democracy, rather than socialism, is subversive."

42. The literature on feminism and Foucault is enormous. Much of it is summarized in Vikki Bell, *Interrogating Incest: Feminism, Foucault, and the Law* (London: Routledge, 1993), and in Linda J. Nicholson, ed., *Feminism/Postmodernism* (New York: Routledge, 1990).

43. Foucault posed the same question in terms of the repressive hypothesis in *The History of Sexuality*, vol. 1, *An Introduction* (New York: Vintage/Random House, 1980). See the passages on the "speaker's benefit" (6–7) and "the ease of acceptance" (86).

44. Charles Murray, *Losing Ground: American Social Policy, 1950–1980* (New York: Basic Books, 1984), 9.

45. Ibid., 217.

46. Ibid., 217.

47. Richard J. Herrnstein and Charles Murray, *The Bell Curve: Intelligence and Class Structure in American Life* (New York: Free Press, 1994).

48. Theresa Funiciello, *The Tyranny of Kindness: Dismantling the Welfare System to End Poverty in America* (New York: Atlantic Monthly Press, 1993), 119.

49. See Iris Marion Young, "Punishment, Treatment, Empowerment: Three Approaches to Policy for Pregnant Addicts," *Feminist Studies* 20 (Spring 1994): 33–57.

50. One such program in Minneapolis, called TLC, was conducted and funded by a network of agencies and corporations: United Way, Honeywell, Success by Six, Year of the City, FAO Schwartz, and the Minneapolis Health Department. They offered things "women wouldn't buy for themselves," such as movie tickets and dinners.

51. The phrase comes from the title of Funiciello's chap. 6 in *Tyranny of Kindness*.

52. It is on this point that I differ with Kathy Ferguson's excellent *The Feminist Case against Bureaucracy* (Philadelphia: Temple University Press, 1984); see esp. xv, 150–52. She distinguishes clearly between citizens (welfare activists) and subjects (compliant recipients), and she understands welfare to be an institution of social domination and control.

53. The logic of liberal democratic government can seem somewhat relentless. Consider "A Source for Empowerment: The Family Violence Program at Bedford Hills Correctional Facility," a report issued by the State of New York, Department of Correctional Services, in May 1994: "Through the program the participants have developed insight into the causes or nature of their self-destructive behavior. They have gained the strength and ability to redirect their lives into more appropriate, goal-directed activities. A solidarity exists among the participants. A special rapport has been developed with the staff" (2). Here, even a prison can be transformed into a place of "empowerment." Thanks to Mariana Valverde for alerting me to the report.

54. Michel Foucault, *The History of Sexuality: Volume One, An Introduction* (New York: Vintage Books, 1980): 143.

55. Nikolas Rose, *Governing the Soul: The Shaping of the Private Self* (London: Routledge, 1990).

56. Foucault, "Governmentality," in *The Foucualt Effect: Studies in Governmentality*, ed. Graham Burchell, Colin Gordon, and Peter Miller (Chicago: University of Chicago Press, 1992), 102.

57. Iris Young argues that treatment meted out to pregnant addicts "often operates to adjust women to the dominant gender, race, and class strucures and depoliticizes and individualizes their situations" ("Punishment, Treatment, Empowerment," 33–34). I argue to the contrary that treatment governmentalizes their situations.

Nancy J. Hirschmann, "Domestic Violence and the Theoretical Discourse of Freedom," *Frontiers* 26, no.1 (1996): 126–51, considers the policies for treating a victim of domestic violence to claim that liberal discourses of freedom are inadequate and to examine the material construction of the "choice" to leave her batterer.

58. Nancy Fraser, *Unruly Practices: Power, Discourse, and Gender in Contemporary Social Theory* (Minneapolis: University of Minnesota Press, 1989), esp. chap. 7.

59. Foucault, "Governmentality," 89.

60. Foucault, "The Subject and Power," 221.

61. Samuel Delany's novel *The Mad Man* appears in several different revised editions. The quotation is taken from a brilliant review of Delany's pornographic novels by Ray Davis, "Delany's Dirt," in *Ash of Stars: On the Writing of Samuel R. Delany*, ed. James Sallis (Oxford: University Press of Mississippi, 1996), 179.

CHAPTER 2. THE LIBERAL ARTS OF GOVERNANCE

1. Arguments to revive civil society as the space of autonomy are proliferating at the moment. For critical summaries, see Michael J. Shapiro, "Bowling Blind: Post Liberal Civil Society and the Worlds of Neo-Tocquevillian Social Theory," *Theory and Event* 1, no.1 (1995) (http://128.220.50.88/journals/theory_&_event/v001/1.1shapiro.html); Nikolas Rose, "Between Authority and Liberty: Governing Virtue in a Free Society," forthcoming in *Janus: The Journal of the Finnish Society for Social Policy* (1998); Michael Hardt, "The Withering of Civil Society," *Social Text* 14 (Winter 1995): 27–44. Also, for a defense of civil society, see Michael Walzer, "The Idea of Civil Society: A Path to Social Reconstruction," *Dissent*, Spring 1991, 293–304.

2. Adam Ferguson, *An Essay on the History of Civil Society* (1767; Cambridge: Cambridge University Press, 1995). Ferguson is noted as one of the first to use the term "civilization." He is also sometimes held to be, along with other figures of the Scottish Enlightenment, one of the first sociologists. My reading of Ferguson draws upon Colin Gordon, "Governmental Rationality: An Introduction," and Graham Burchell, "Peculiar Interests: Civil Society and Governing the 'System of Natural Liberty,'" both in *The Foucault Effect: Studies in Governmentality*, ed. Graham Burchell, Colin Gordon, and Peter Miller (Chicago: University of Chicago Press, 1991).

3. See Gordon, "Governmental Rationality."

4. Adam Ferguson quoted in Fania Oz-Salzberger's introduction to Ferguson, *Essay on the History of Civil Society*, xxiii.

5. Michel Foucault, "Governmentality," in Burchell, Gordon, and Miller, *The Foucault Effect*.

6. Bruno Latour, "The Powers of Association," in *Power, Action, and Belief: A New Sociology of Knowledge?* ed. John Law (New York: Routledge, 1986), 269. In addition to Foucault's essays cited here, see Mary Poovey, *Making a Social Body: British Cultural Formation, 1830–1864* (Chicago: University of Chicago Press, 1995).

7. The classic statement on negative and positive liberty is made by Isaiah Berlin, *Four Essays on Liberty* (Oxford: Oxford University Press, 1969).

8. T. H. Green, *Lectures on the Principles of Political Obligation and Other Writings*, ed. Paul Harris and John Murrow (1895; Cambridge: Cambridge University Press, 1986), 89.

9. Cf. Isaiah Berlin's warning (*Four Essays*, 118–172) that positive liberty forces one to be free.

10. Green, *Lectures*, 264. Self-help was not always a technique for "the conduct of conduct." For example, in 1859, Samuel Smiles provided a series of character studies to teach self-help by example. He wrote a traditional conduct book, in other words, one that did not suggest any mode of acting upon others. See Smiles, *Self-Help* (1859; London: John Murray Ltd., 1969). For a thorough re-thinking of Berlin's distinction between negative and positive liberty, see Duncan Ivison, *The Self at Liberty: Political Argument and the Arts of Government* (Ithaca, N.Y.: Cornell University Press, 1997).

11. Ibid., 161.

12. Ibid., 162.

13. Ibid., 94.

14. Octavia Hill, "A Few Words to Volunteer Visitors among the Poor," in *Our Common Land* (London: Macmillan, 1877), 54.

15. Hill, *Our Common Land*, 57.

16. Octavia Hill, "A More Excellent Way of Charity," in *Our Common Land*, 83.

17. Poovey, *Making a Social Body*, 47.

18. Hill, *Our Common Land*, 61–62.

19. Quoted in Gertrude Himmelfarb, *Poverty and Compassion: The Moral Imagination of the Late Victorians* (New York: Vintage, 1991), 214.

20. Hill, *Our Common Land*, 36.

21. Ibid., 26–27.

22. Ibid., 40.

23. Helen Bosanquet, *Rich and Poor* (London: Macmillan, 1908), 40–41.

24. Ibid., 53.

25. Helen Bosanquet, *The Standard of Life* (New York: Macmillan, 1906), 278.

26. Ibid., 17.

27. Ibid., 1.

28. Ibid., 2.

29. Ibid., 41.

30. On indirect government, see Nikolas Rose and Peter Miller, "Political Power beyond the State: Problematics of Government," *British Journal of Sociology* 43 (June 1992): 1–31.

31. Bosanquet, *Standard of Life*, 195.

32. Sheldon Wolin's thesis that political orders are reconstituted in times of crisis is treated in Kirstie McClure, "The Issue of Foundations: Scientized Politics, Politicized Science, and Feminist Critical Practice," in *Feminists Theorize the Political*, ed. Judith Butler and Joan Scott (New York: Routledge, 1992), 341–68.

33. Michel Foucault, "The Subject and Power," in *Michel Foucault: Beyond Structuralism and Hermeneutics*, 2d ed., ed. Hubert L. Dreyfus and Paul Rabinow (Chicago: University of Chicago Press, 1983), 221.

34. Hannah Fenichel Pitkin, "Conformism, Housekeeping, and the Attack of the Blob: The Origins of Hannah Arendt's Concept of the Social," in *Feminist Interpretations of Hannah Arendt*, ed. Bonnie Honig (University Station: Pennsylvania State University Press, 1995), 51–82. Many of the themes in Arendt's work which I discuss are given more suggestive and sympathetic attention in Honig's collection than I give them here.

35. Hannah Arendt, *The Human Condition* (Chicago: University of Chicago Press, 1958), 33 n 24.

36. Ibid., 40.

37. Ibid.

38. Ibid., 47.

39. Ibid., 28, 35.

40. Ibid., 21.

41. Ibid., 41.

42. The best treatments of Arendt's work on the question of democracy are Hanna Fenichel Pitkin, "Justice: On Relating Public and Private," *Political Theory* 9 (1981): 327–52; and the essays in Honig, *Feminist Interpretations of Hannah Arendt*.

43. "The space of appearance comes into being wherever men are together in the manner of speech and action, and therefore predates and precedes all formal constitution of the public realm and the various forms of government. . . . it does not survive the actuality of the movement which brought it into being" (Arendt, *The Human Condition*, 199).

44. See William Connolly, *The Ethos of Pluralization* (Minneapolis: University of Minnesota Press, 1995).

45. Beatrice Webb cited in Judith Walkowitz's excellent history of women's involvement in the public sphere, *City of Dreadful Delight: Narratives of Sexual Danger in Late-Victorian London* (Chicago: University of Chicago Press, 1992), 57.

46. I am drawing again from the wonderful history of garbage reform by Martin V. Melosi, *Garbage in the Cities: Refuse, Reform, and the Environment, 1890–1980* (Chicago: Dorsey Press, 1981), 119. Virtually the same comment was made by Comte; see Denise Riley, *"Am I That Name?" Feminism and the Category of "Women" in History* (Minneapolis: University of Minnesota Press, 1988), 49.

47. Denise Riley (ibid., 49) sums up the emergence of the social as follows: "The nineteenth century 'social' is the reiterated sum of progressive philanthropies, theories of class, of poverty, of degeneration; studies of the domestic lives of workers, their housing, hygiene, morality, mortality; of their exploitation, or their need for protection, as this bore on their family lives too. It is a blurred ground between the old public and pri-

vate, voiced as a field for intervention, love, and reform by socialists, conservatives, radicals, liberals, and feminists in their different and conjoined ways. . . . Once the seemingly neutral and vacant backdrop of "the social" presents itself for scrutiny, it appears as a strange phenomenon in its own right."

48. Ibid., 48.

49. Riley's account of women and the social does not simply laud the accomplishments of feminist reformers but points out how middle-class women came to occupy the entire category "women" to the exclusion of working-class and minority women. Her contribution to feminist theory is an explanation of how the social both enabled and constrained women's activism. Compare the recent celebration of middle-class women's contribution to the social in Theda Skocpol, *Protecting Soldiers and Mothers: The Political Origins of Social Policy in the United States* (Cambridge: Harvard University Press, 1992).

Also important is the debate that followed the publication of Jacque Donzelot, *The Policing of Families* (New York: Pantheon, 1990). See Michele Barrett and Mary McIntosh, *The Anti-Social Family*, 2d ed. (London: Verso, 1982), esp. 95–104 and 161–72; and Paul Hirst, "The Genesis of the Social," *Politics & Power Three*, 1981: 67–95. In a related exchange, Joan Scott and Linda Gordon debated the historical terms of women's agency in relation to the social; see *Signs* 15, no. 4 (Summer 1990): 848–60.

50. In addition to the works already cited, see, e.g., Lori D. Ginzberg, *Women and the Work of Benevolence: Morality, Politics, and Class in the 19th-Century United States* (New Haven: Yale University Press, 1990); Linda Gordon, *Heroes of Their Own Lives: The Politics and History of Family Violence* (New York: Penguin, 1988); Judith Walkowitz, *Prostitution and Victorian Society: Women, Class, and the State* (Cambridge: Cambridge University Press, 1980).

51. Nancy Fraser, *Unruly Practices: Power, Discourse, and Gender in Contemporary Social Theory* (Minneapolis: University of Minnesota Press, 1989), and *Justice Interruptus: Critical Reflections on the "Postsocialist" Condition* (New York: Routledge, 1997); Wendy Brown, *States of Injury: Power and Freedom in Late Modernity* (Princeton: Princeton University Press, 1995), 3.

52. Fraser, *Unruly Practices*, 175–81.

53. Ibid., 177.

54. Graham Burchell makes a related claim in, "Liberal Government and Techniques of the Self," in *Foucault and Political Reason: Liberalism, Neo-Liberalism, and Rationalities of Government*, ed. Andrew Barry, Thomas Osborne, and Nikolas Rose (London: University College London Press, 1996), 19–36.

55. Brown, *States of Injury*, 15.

56. Ibid., 173. Brown refers to Barbara Ehrenreich and Frances Fox Piven, "Women of the Welfare State," in *Alternatives: Proposals for America from the Democratic Left*, ed. Irving Howe (New York: Pantheon, 1983).

57. Frances Fox Piven, "Ideology and the State: Women, Power, and the Welfare State," in *Women, the State, and Welfare*, ed. Linda Gordon (Madison: University of Wisconsin Press, 1990), 250–51.

58. Walkowitz, *Prostitution and Victorian Society*.

59. See, e.g., Pat Califia, *Public Sex: The Culture of Radical Sex* (Pittsburgh: Cleis,

1994); and Lisa Duggan and Nan Hunter, *Sex Wars: Sexual Dissent and Political Culture* (New York: Routledge, 1995).

60. Samuel P. Huntington, "The United States," in *The Crisis of Democracy: Report on the Governability of Democracies to the Trilateral Commission*, ed. Michael Crozier, Samuel P. Huntington, and Joji Watanuki (New York: New York University Press, 1975), 112.

61. Ibid., 64.

62. Ibid., 4.

63. Ibid., 5.

64. Ibid., 84.

65. Ibid., 6.

66. Ibid., 75.

67. Ibid., 7.

68. Ibid., 75.

69. Ibid., 9.

70. Brzezinski quoted in ibid., 7.

71. Jürgen Habermas similarly read the signs of political life to signal a "breakdown" of the public sphere: "Two tendencies dialectically related to each other indicated a breakdown of the public sphere. While it penetrated more *spheres* of society, it simultaneously lost its *political* function, namely: that of subjecting the affairs that it had made public to the control of a critical public." (*The Structural Transformation of the Public Sphere*, trans. Thomas Burger with Frederick Lawrence [Boston: MIT Press, 1988], 140).

72. See Ernesto Laclau and Chantal Mouffe, *Hegemony and Socialist Strategy: Towards a Radical Democratic Politics* (London: Verso, 1985).

73. Arendt, *The Human Condition*, 45.

74. Ian Hacking, "Making Up People," in *Reconstructing Individualism: Autonomy, Individuality, and the Self in Western Thought*, ed. Thomas Heller (Palo Alto, Calif.: Stanford University Press, 1986), 223.

CHAPTER 3. THE WILL TO EMPOWER

1. Where "the poor" appears in quotation marks, I mean to highlight the fact that the category was an administrative invention of the antipoverty programs. Where the term does not appear in quotation marks, I mean to indicate that the coherence of the group was accepted as a fact.

2. Peter L. Berger and Richard John Neuhaus, *To Empower People: The Role of Mediating Structures in Public Policy* (Washington, D.C.: American Enterprise Institute for Public Policy Research, 1977), 3. On Kemp and Darman, see Daniel Wattenberg, "'Power to the People' Becomes a Young Republican War Cry," *Insight on the News*, vol. 6, no.52 (Dec. 24, 1990), 18.

3. Cf., e.g., Lawrence Mead, *Beyond Entitlement: The Social Obligations of Citizenship* (New York: Free Press, 1986), and Theresa Funiciello, *The Tyranny of Kindness: Dismantling the Welfare System to End Poverty in America* (New York: Atlantic Monthly Press, 1993).

4. Ann Bookman and Sandra Morgen, eds., *Women and the Politics of Empowerment* (Philadelphia: Temple University Press, 1988), 4.

5. Jacqueline Pope, "The Colonizing Impact of Public Service Bureaucracies in Black Communities," in *Race, Politics, and Economic Development: Community Perspectives,* ed. James Jennings (New York: Verso, 1992), 142.

6. Ibid., 143.

7. The best history of Community Action is by Peter Marris and Martin Rein, *Dilemmas of Social Reform: Poverty and Community Action in the United States,* 2d ed. (Chicago: Aldine, 1967); I have drawn much historical material and insight from their book. See also Alan Altshuler, *Community Control: The Black Demand for Participation in Large American Cities* (New York: Pegasus, 1970); Campaign for Human Development, *Poverty In America: A Study of Social Power* (Washington, D.C.: United States Catholic Conference, 1974); John C. Donovan, *The Politics of Poverty* (New York: Pegasus, 1967); Ralph Kramer, *Participation of the Poor: Comparative Studies in the War on Poverty* (Englewood Cliffs, N.J.: Prentice-Hall, 1969); Stephen M. Rose, *The Betrayal of the Poor: The Transformation of Community Action* (Cambridge, Mass.: Schenkman, 1972).

8. Office of Economic Opportunity, *Community Action Program Guide,* vol. 1 (Washington, D.C.: Office of Economic Opportunity, 1965), 7.

9. George Brager quoted in Marris and Rein, *Dilemmas of Social Reform,* 49.

10. For an earlier account of the invention of the "delinquent," see Anthony Platt, *The Child Savers: The Invention of Delinquency* (Chicago: University of Chicago Press, 1969).

11. Marris and Rein, *Dilemmas of Social Reform,* 24.

12. Quoted in ibid., 36–37.

13. Peter Bachrach, Morton S. Baratz, and Margaret Levi, "The Political Significance of Citizen Participation," in *Power and Poverty: Theory and Practice,* ed. Bachrach and Baratz (New York: Oxford University Press, 1970), 206–7.

14. Senate Committee on Labor and Public Welfare, Subcommittee on Employment, Manpower, and Poverty, *Economic Opportunity Amendments of 1967,* 90th Cong., 1st sess., 1967, Report 563, 20.

15. See, e.g., Daniel Patrick Moynihan's account of CAP in *Maximum Feasible Misunderstanding: Community Action in the War on Poverty* (New York: Free Press, 1970), in which he claims that the poor were manipulated into carrying out the radical agenda of CAP organizers.

16. Office of Economic Opportunity, *Community Action Program Guide,* 1:16.

17. Marris and Rein, *Dilemmas of Social Reform,* 216.

18. Tom Hayden, "Welfare Liberalism and Social Change," rpt. from *Dissent,* in *The Great Society Reader: The Failure of American Liberalism,* ed. Marvin E. Gettleman and David Mermelstein (New York: Vintage, 1987), 478.

19. Ibid., 478.

20. Ibid., 496.

21. An excellent case study of a Manhattan neighborhood is Ira Katznelson, *City Trenches: Urban Politics and the Patterning of Class in the United States* (Chicago: University of Chicago Press, 1981). Katznelson argues that CAPs and programs like them, de-

vised in response to urban uprising and riots, in effect "absorbed the energies of insurgents, ... transformed their protests and rendered them harmless. These institutions did so by reconnecting the disaffected to political life and in this way making them part of the regular, legitimate, and predictable political process" (179–80). His thesis then, is the opposite of mine, that the co-optation of citizens in revolt was designed as a strategy to demobilize civil rights and black power insurgents as well as to deemphasize the politics of class. The effect of programs was to produce political stability and the demobilization of insurgents, according to Katznelson, whereas I argue that political conflict was produced by the mobilization of "the poor." These are clearly related arguments.

22. Nikolas Rose has shown that government is dependent upon knowledge: "To govern a population one needs to isolate it as a sector of reality, to identify certain characteristics and processes proper to it, to make its features notable, speakable, writable, to account for them according to certain explanatory schemes. Government thus depends upon the production, circulation, organization of truths that incarnate what is to be governed, which make it thinkable, calculable, and practicable" (*Governing the Soul: The Shaping of the Private Self* [London: Routledge, 1990], 6).

23. Ibid.

24. Michael Harrington, *The Other America: Poverty in the United States* (New York: Penguin, 1963), 156.

25. It was another best-seller at the time that originated the culture-of-poverty thesis: Oscar Lewis, *The Children of Sanchez* (New York: Random House, 1961). For a critical account of that thesis, see Carol B. Stack, *All Our Kin: Strategies for Survival in a Black Community* (New York: Harper & Row, 1974). Stack illustrates community networks of exchange and help in a poor black community which belie the notion that the poor are powerless. Nonetheless, she argues that welfare works to create and maintain dependency and forecloses class mobility as it buys the acquiescence of welfare recipients: "Welfare programs merely act as flexible mechanisms to alleviate the more obvious symptoms of poverty while inching forward just enough to purchase acquiescence and silence on the part of the members of this class and their liberal supporters. . . . In fact [these programs] are purveyors of the status quo, staunch defenders of the economic imperative that demands maintenance of a sizeable but docile impoverished class" (128). Thus, Stack concurs that welfare programs exclude the authentic participation of recipients, whereas I argue that welfare works by mobilizing certain kinds of participation and action.

26. Harrington, *The Other America*, 21–22.

27. Sargent Shriver, "The War on Poverty Is a Movement of Conscience," in Gettleman and Mermelstein, *The Great Society Reader*, 207.

28. Harrington, *The Other America*, 164.

29. Bachrach, Baratz, and Levi, "Political Significance of Citizen Participation," 206.

30. Marris and Rein, *Dilemmas of Social Reform*, 44.

31. Office of Economic Opportunity, *Organizing Communities for Action under the 1967 Amendment to the Economic Opportunity Act* (Washington, D.C.: Office of Economic Opportunity, 1968), 4.

32. Ibid., 7.

33. Marris and Rein, *Dilemmas of Social Reform*, 229.

34. Kramer, *Participation of the Poor*, 265.

35. Michel Foucault, "The Subject and Power," in *Michel Foucault: Beyond Structuralism and Hermeneutics*, 2d. ed., ed. Hubert L. Dreyfus and Paul Rabinow (Chicago: University of Chicago Press, 1983), 225.

36. Kramer, *Participation of the Poor*, 247.

37. Grant McConnell quoted in Althshuler, *Community Control*, 77.

38. Similarities between pluralist and Foucauldian notions of power have been noted (and overstated) in Fred Dallmayr, *Polis and Praxis: Exercises in Contemporary Political Theory* (Cambridge, Mass.: MIT Press, 1984).

39. Foucault, "The Subject and Power," 220.

40. Peter Bachrach and Morton S. Baratz, "The Two Faces of Power," *American Political Science Review* 56 (1970): 947–52.

41. See, e.g., John Gaventa, *Power and Powerlessness: Quiescence and Rebellion in an Appalachian Valley* (Urbana: University of Illinois Press, 1980); David Couzens Hoy, "Power, Repression, Progress: Foucault, Lukes, and the Frankfurt School," in *Foucault: A Critical Reader*, ed. David Couzens Hoy (Oxford: Basil Blackwell, 1986); and Peter Miller, *Domination and Power* (London: Routledge, 1987).

42. Marris and Rein, *Dilemmas of Social Reform*, 222.

43. Bachrach, Baratz, and Levi, "Political Significance of Citizen Participation," *Power and Poverty*, 207.

44. Hayden, "Welfare Liberalism," 496.

45. See, e.g., Francis Fox Piven and Richard A. Cloward, *Poor People's Movements: Why They Succeed, How They Fail* (New York: Vintage, 1979), and *Regulating the Poor: The Functions of Public Welfare* (New York: Pantheon, 1971).

CHAPTER 4. REVOLUTIONS WITHIN

1. Gloria Steinem, *Revolution from Within: A Book of Self-Esteem* (Boston: Little, Brown, 1992).

2. Deidre English, review of *Revolution from Within* by Gloria Steinem, *New York Times Book Review*, February 2, 1992, 13.

3. Nikolas Rose, "Beyond the Public/Private Division: Law, Power, and the Family," *Journal of Law and Society* 14 (Spring 1987): 61–76. Rose offers a compelling account of the limitations of feminist critique based on the public/private division which has influenced my arguments here.

4. California Task Force to Promote Self-Esteem and Personal and Social Responsibility, *Appendixes to "Toward a State of Esteem"* (Sacramento: California Department of Education, 1990), 102.

5. California Task Force to Promote Self-Esteem and Personal and Social Responsibility, *Toward a State of Esteem: The Final Report* (Sacramento: California Department of Education, 1990), vii–viii.

6. Ibid., 22.

7. Ibid., 4.

8. Ibid., vii.

9. Ian Hacking, "Making Up People," in *Reconstructing Individualism: Autonomy, Individuality, and the Self in Western Thought,* ed. Thomas Heller, Morton Sosna, and David E. Wellbery (Palo Alto, Calif.: Stanford University Press, 1986). Consider, for example, the following titles listed in California Task Force, *State of Esteem;* Stewart Emery, *Actualizations: You Don't Have to Rehearse to Be Yourself* (New York: Irving, 1980); Morris Rosenberg, *Conceiving the Self* (Melbourne, Fla.: Robert E. Krieger, 1979); Virginia Satir, *People Making* (Palo Alto, Calif.: Science & Behavior Books, 1988).

10. California Task Force, *State of Esteem,* ix.

11. Steinem, *Revolution from Within,* 29.

12. Michel Foucault, "The Political Technology of Individuals," in *Technologies of the Self,* ed. Luther H. Martin, Huck Gutman, and Patrick H. Hutton (Amherst, Mass.: University of Massachusetts Press, 1988), 146.

13. California Task Force, *Appendixes,* 102.

14. California Task Force, *State of Esteem,* 22.

15. Andrew Mecca, Neil Smelser, and John Vasconellos, eds., *The Social Importance of Self-Esteem* (Berkeley: University of California Press, 1989).

16. Nikolas Rose argues that governing subjectivity is not consistent with centralized power: "Rather, government of subjectivity has taken shape through the proliferation of a complex and heterogeneous assemblage of technologies. These have acted as relays, bringing the varied ambitions of political, scientific, philanthropic, and professional authorities into alignment with the ideals and aspirations of individuals, with the selves each of us wants to be" (*Governing the Soul: The Shaping of the Private Self* [London: Routledge, 1990], 213).

17. See Michel Foucault, "The Subject and Power," in *Michel Foucault: Beyond Structuralism and Hermeneutics,* 2d ed., ed. Hubert L. Dreyfus and Paul Rabinow (Chicago: University of Chicago Press, 1983).

18. Rose, *Governing the Soul,* 256.

19. Ibid., 213.

20. Mecca, Smelser, and Vasconellos, *Social Importance of Self-Esteem,* 15.

21. Ibid.: "One of the disappointing aspects of every chapter in this volume (at least to those of us who adhere to the intuitively correct models sketched above) is how low the association between self-esteem and its consequences are in research to date." Notice that although no association is established, self-esteem is here linked to "its consequences."

22. California Task Force, *State of Esteem,* 44.

23. Thomas Scheff, Suzanne M. Retzinger, and Michael T. Ryan, "Crime, Violence, and Self-Esteem: Review and Proposals," in Mecca, Smelser, and Vasconellos, *Social Importance of Self-Esteem,* 179.

24. Rose, *Governing the Soul,* 256.

25. Theresa Funiciello's arguments, discussed in Chapter 2, provide a case in point. Although she fails to see that the social services are a form of governing the poor, she does clearly articulate the relationship between the social science professions and in-

come redistribution. From *The Tyranny of Kindness: Dismantling the Welfare System to End Poverty in America* (New York: Atlantic Monthly Press, 1983), 38: "What became the professionalization of being human took off, bloating under government contracts. For every poverty problem, a self-perpetuating profession proposed to ameliorate the situation without altering the poverty."

26. California Task Force, *Appendixes*, 104.

27. Scheff, Retzinger, and Ryan, "Crime, Violence, and Self-Esteem," 192–93.

28. California Task Force, *State of Esteem*, 12.

29. Steinem, *Revolution from Within*, 9–10.

30. Alexis de Tocqueville, *Democracy in America* (New York: Harper Perennial, 1969), 672.

31. Ibid., 510.

32. Ibid., 91.

33. Ibid., 12.

34. Ibid., 517.

35. Ibid., 510.

36. Ibid., 521.

37. Ibid., 517.

38. Ibid., 527.

39. The disciplinary origins of democratic citizenship in the United States are elaborated by Thomas Dumm, *Democracy and Punishment: Disciplinary Origins of the United States* (Madison: University of Wisconsin Press, 1987). Also see Roger Boesche, *The Strange Liberalism of Alexis de Tocqueville* (Ithaca, N.Y.: Cornell University Press, 1987), 229–59.

40. As Peter Miller put it, "Carceral power opened up the entire fabric of society to a normalizing regulation, but it no longer provides the exclusive model" (*Domination and Power* [London: Routledge, 1987], 201).

41. Tocqueville, *Democracy in America*, 667.

42. Ibid., 510.

43. Ibid., 515.

44. Ibid., 72.

45. Ibid., 691.

46. Ibid., 669.

47. Ibid.

48. Ibid., 693.

49. Ibid., 736.

50. Ibid., 694.

51. Gustave de Beaumont and Alexis de Tocqueville, *On the Penitentiary System in the United States and Its Application in France* (Carbondale: Southern Illinois University Press, 1964), 80.

52. California Task Force, *State of Esteem*, 37.

53. Eve Kosofsky Sedgwick uses addiction to illustrate the production of a similiarly pathologized identity on the basis of the subject's lack. See her "Epidemics of

the Will," in *Zone 6: Incorporations*, ed. Jonathon Crary and Sanford Kwinter (New York: Urzone, 1992).

54. Ian Hacking, "Self-Improvement," in *Foucault: A Critical Reader*, ed. David Couzens Hoy (Oxford: Basil Blackwell, 1986), 236.

CHAPTER 5. WELFARE QUEENS

1. Friedrich Wilhelm Nietzsche, *On the Genealogy of Morals*, ed. Walter Kaufman (New York: Vintage, 1967), 45.

2. Lucie White, "Subordination, Rhetorical Survival Skills, and Sunday Shoes: Notes on the Hearing of Mrs. G.," *Buffalo Law Review* 38 (Winter 1990): 37.

3. Frances Fox Piven and Richard A. Cloward, "The Contemporary Relief Debate," in *The Mean Season: The Attack on the Welfare State*, ed. Fred Block et al. (New York: Pantheon, 1987), 48.

4. For some of the historical accounts of welfare rights strategies that I have found useful, see Frances Fox Piven and Richard A. Cloward, *Poor People's Movements: Why They Succeed, How They Fail* (New York: Vintage, 1979); Milwaukee County Welfare Rights Organization, *Welfare Mothers Speak Out: We Ain't Gonna Shuffle Anymore* (New York: Norton, 1972); Mimi Abromovitz, *Regulating the Lives of Women: Social Welfare Policy from Colonial Times to the Present* (Boston: South End Press, 1988); Jackie Pope, "Women in the Welfare Rights Struggle: The Brooklyn Welfare Action Council," in *Women and Social Protest*, ed. Guida West and Rhoda Lois Blumberg (New York: Oxford University Press, 1990), 57–74.

5. Kathryn Edin and Laura Lein, *Making Ends Meet: How Single Mothers Survive Welfare and Low-Wage Work* (New York: Russell Sage Foundation, 1997). Strangely enough (or, actually, predictably in the terms of my own argument), Edin and Lein's work is sympathtic to welfare recipients.

6. Judith Butler, *Gender Trouble: Feminism and the Subversion of Identity* (New York: Routledge, 1990), 2.

7. Nancy Fraser, "Struggle over Needs: Outline of a Socialist-Feminist Critical Theory of Late-Capitalist Political Culture," in *Women, the State, and Welfare*, ed. Linda Gordon (Madison: University of Wisconsin Press, 1990), 199–225.

8. "Relations of rule" is a phrase from Dorothy Smith, cited in Chandra Mohanty, "Cartographies of Struggle: Third World Feminism and the Politics of Feminism," in *Third World Women and the Politics of Feminism*, ed. Mohanty, Ann Russo, and Lourdes Torres (Bloomington: Indiana University Press, 1991). Mohanty suggests that a politics of location can in strategic ways replace the politics of representation and identity.

9. "Waste, fraud, abuse, and error," a list of equivalents constituting a "crisis," comes from a conference held in 1978 by then HEW Secretary Joseph Califano; see U.S. Department of Health, Education, and Welfare, *Conference Proceedings, The Secretary's National Conference on Fraud, Abuse, and Error: Protecting the Taxpayer's Dollar* (Washington, D.C.: Department of Health, Education, and Welfare, 1979).

10. On freedom and liberal government, see Thomas L. Dumm, *Democracy and Punishment: Disciplinary Origins of the United States* (Madison: University of Wisconsin Press, 1987), and *Michel Foucault and the Politics of Freedom* (Thousand Oaks, Calif.: Sage, 1996).

11. White, "Subordination," 43.

12. See Robert W. Collin and Willa M. Hemmons, "Equal Protection Problems with Welfare Fraud Prosecution," *Loyola Law Review* 33 (Spring 1987): 17–49.

13. Wahneema Lubiano, "Black Ladies, Welfare Queens, and State Minstrels: Ideological War by Narrative Means," in *Race-ing Justice, En-Gendering Power: Essays on Anita Hill, Clarence Thomas, and the Construction of Social Reality*, ed. Toni Morrison (New York: Pantheon, 1992), 340.

14. Nikolas Rose, "Governing by Numbers: Figuring Out Democracy," *Accounting, Organizations, and Society* 16, no. 7 (1991): 673–92.

15. Quoted in Evelyn Z. Brodkin, *The False Promise of Administrative Reform: Implementing Quality Control in Welfare* (Philadelpia: Temple University Press, 1986), 25.

16. Brodkin, *False Promise*; Michael Lipsky, "Bureaucratic Disentitlement in Social Welfare Programs," *Social Service Review*, 58 (March 1984): 3–27.

17. Brodkin, *False Promise*, 30.

18. Jimmy Carter quoted in John A. Gardiner and Theodore R. Lyman, *The Fraud Control Game: State Responses to Fraud and Abuse in AFDC and Medicaid Programs* (Bloomington: Indiana University Press, 1984), 2.

19. Ibid., 10.

20. Department of Health, Education, and Welfare, *Conference Proceedings*.

21. See Lipsky, "Bureaucratic Disentitlement"; and Brodkin, *False Promise*.

22. For a compelling and detailed account of one administrative hearing, see White, "Subordination." Many thanks to Austin Sarat for pointing out White's article to me.

23. E.g., Gardiner and Lyman (*Fraud Control Game*, 1984) report that "administrative sanctions" can be used to bypass the criminal justice system so that fines of 25 percent can be administratively imposed on top of the excess assistance which a recipient must repay. That is, the recipient must recoup any grant monies *and* pay fines or interest on overpayments, even if the overpayment was caused by agency error and no fraud has been proved. Also see General Accounting Office, *Benefit Overpayments: Recoveries Could Be Increased in the Food Stamp and AFDC Programs* (Washington, D.C.: U.S. General Accounting Office, 1986), a report that advocates stepping up administrative recoupments (even in cases of agency error) rather than criminal prosecutions for fraud.

24. Brodkin, *False Promise*.

25. Rose, "Governing by Numbers," 678–79.

26. Sheldon Wolin, "Democracy and the Welfare State: The Political and Theoretical Connections between *Staatsrason* and *Wohlfahrtsstaatsrason*," in *The Presence of the Past: Essays on the State and the Constitution* (Baltimore: Johns Hopkins University Press, 1989), 160.

27. White, ("Subordination," 39 n.12), while representing AFDC claimants, observed that "workers are trained to emphasize fraud at each stage in the application and

grant review process. Claimants are subject to repeated lectures from their workers about fraud, and must sign forms acknowledging that they have understood those warnings. In addition, they must submit third party verifications of virtually all the information they provide in the application process. . . . The only justification offered to clients for these requirements is to prevent them from committing fraud."

28. The forms I use here are published by the Minnesota Department of Human Services: for example, DHS-1842 (3–87) PZ-01842-05.

29. Following the Debt Reduction Act of 1984, a public information flyer printed by the Minnesota Department of Human Services in June 1987, titled, "Notice About I.E.V.S. [Income and Eligibility Verification System]," listed these agencies. A 1990 flyer, "Your Privacy Rights" listed social services.

30. In the case of Mrs. G (White, "Subordination," 32), an administrative judge decided against her; then, after she filed an appeal, the county welfare director called her lawyer to say that "the county had decided that it wouldn't be 'fair' to make Mrs. G pay the money back." No explanation was given.

31. Lipsky, 15.

32. Bruno Latour, "The Powers of Association," in *Power, Action, and Belief: A New Sociology of Knowledge?* ed. John Law (New York: Routledge, 1986).

33. Jim Torczyner, "Discretion, Judgment, and Informed Consent: Ethical and Practice Issues in Social Action," *Social Work* 36 (March 1991): 124.

34. Nikolas Rose and Peter Miller, "Political Power beyond the State: Problematics of Government," *British Journal of Sociology* 43:2 (June 1992): 173–205.

35. Forgive the fact that my case is articulated against the critical and politically engaged writings of Nancy Fraser. The negative attention I give her writing here is a measure of how well her own work has measured up to the possibilities of political theory. Fraser, "Struggle over Needs," 213–19.

36. Carol Stack, *All Our Kin: Strategies for Survival in a Black Community* (New York: Harper & Row, 1974).

37. Fraser, "Struggle over Needs," 219.

38. Wendy Brown, who is both critical of identity politics and sympathetic to prioritizing "the political," poses the state as the center of resistance in *States of Injury: Power and Freedom in Late Modernity* (Princeton: Princeton University Press, 1995).

39. Fraser, "Struggle over Needs," 219.

40. Ibid., 204.

41. Francis Fox Piven and Richard A. Cloward, *The New Class War: Reagan's Attack on the Welfare State and Its Consequences* (New York: Pantheon, 1982), 6 (my emphasis).

42. Milwaukee County Welfare Rights Organization, *Welfare Mothers Speak Out.*

43. Jacqueline Urla suggests that numbers themselves may be used as tools of resistance; see her "Cultural Politics in an Age of Statistics: Numbers, Nations, and the Making of Basque Identity," *American Ethnologist* 20, no. 4 (1993): 818–43.

44. Michel Foucault, "The Subject and Power," in *Michel Foucault: Beyond Structuralism and Hermeneutics*, 2d ed., ed. Hubert L. Dreyfus and Paul Rabinow (Chicago: University of Chicago Press, 1983), 216.

1. Nikolas Rose, "Between Authority and Liberty: Governing Virtue in a Free Society," *Janus: The Journal of the Finnish Society for Social Policy* (forthcoming). See the essays by Michael Shapiro and Nikolas Rose cited earlier.

2. Robert D. Putnam, "Tuning In, Tuning Out: The Strange Disappearance of Social Capital in America," *PS: Political Science & Politics*, December 1995, 664–65.

3. Samuel Delany, "The Rhetoric of Sex and the Discourse of Desire," in *Heterotopia: Postmodern Utopia and the Body Politic*, ed. Tobin Siebers (Ann Arbor: Michigan University Press, 1994), 229–72.

Index

Riley, Denise, 59, 135–136
Rose, Nikolas, 127, 132–134, 139–141,
    144–146
    social science, 76, 110, 113

Scott, Joan, 127, 130, 136
Second Harvest, 128
Sedgwick, Eve, 23, 142
self-esteem, 6, 87–103
self-help, 48–54, 73–86
Shapiro, Michael, 133, 146
Smelser, Neil, 92–93
Smiles, Samuel, 134
social
    "housekeeping," 58–62
    invention of, 43–66
social capital, 122–123
social conduct, 7–9
social control, 30–44, 54–58
    and administrative reform, 110–121
    and Community Action Programs, 76,
        80–86
    and theories of power, 30–42
social movements, new, 62–66
    and disciplinary power, 87–103
    See also social reform movements
social reform movements, 6, 48–54
    Charity Organization Society, 48–54,
        66, 107
    Community Action Programs, 67–86
    empowerment zones, 68
    Female Bible Mission, 49–50
    Great Society, 34–36, 67–86
    Mobilization for Youth, 73–74
    sanitation reform, 8–18, 58–59
    self-esteem, 87–103
    Social Purity, 61
    Tennessee Valley Authority, 84
    welfare rights, 115–121, 143
social science,
    constitutive role of, 76–84, 89–95

social services,
    class interests of, 34–42
"society as a whole," 6–8
Stack, Carol B., 139, 145
Steinem, Gloria, 87–103, 140–142
subjects, 19–42, 85–86

technologies of citizenship, 1–9
    empowerment, 67–86
    See also self-help
Tocqueville, Alexis de, 1, 19–24, 57, 87,
    142
    science of association, 96–103
Trilateral Commission, 62–66

Up & Out of Poverty Now, 13
Urla, Jacqueline, 145

Vasconcellos, John, 90, 141

Walkowitz, Judith, 61, 135–136
Waring, George Edwin, 8–10, 25, 50, 122,
    127
War on Poverty. See social reform
    movements, Great Society
Wattenberg, Daniel, 137
Webb, Beatrice, 58–60, 135
welfare
    feminist theories of, 58–61
    fraud, 104–121
    quality control, 111–115
    and social control, 31–42
White, Lucie, 105–108, 143–144
Wiley, George, 61, 121
Wolin, Sheldon, 130–131, 135, 144
    citizenship, 24–34
    depoliticization, 26–28, 64
    welfare, 113
Women, Work, and Welfare, 118

Young, Iris Marion, 130–133